CHAMP
WILD

*AN ACTION-PACKED ANIMAL OLYMPICS
ADVENTURE*

Cole Wilder

First Edition

ISBN: 9798278106401

Dedication

For Myers and Caleb,
and for every kid who reads this book.
Every animal has a strength.
May you always know yours.

TABLE OF CONTENTS

Chapter 1 – Opening Ceremonies 2

Chapter 2 – 100 Meter Dash 11

Chapter 3 – High Jump 18

Chapter 4 – 50 Meter Swim 27

Chapter 5 – Burrowing Speed Race 35

Chapter 6 – Strength Lift 44

Chapter 7 – Endurance Marathon 53

Chapter 8 – Aerial Acrobatics 62

Chapter 9 – Precision Pecking 70

Chapter 10 – Long Jump 78

Chapter 11 – Team Relay Race 85

Chapter 12 – Tug-Of-War 94

Chapter 13 – Ice Slide Race 103

Chapter 14 – Climbing Competition 112

Chapter 15 – Loudest Call 122

Chapter 16 – Obstacle Course 130

Chapter 17 – Navigation Race 141

Chapter 18 – Closing Ceremonies 152

1 — THE OPENING CEREMONIES

I've commented on hundreds of games, races, and ridiculous backyard competitions involving flying squirrels and stolen birdseed.

But I've never seen *anything* like this.

"Good evening, world!" I shout into my headset, trying not to puff my chest out too far. "This is Coach Talon, broadcasting live from the very first Animal Olympics Stadium, where the air is electric, the fur is brushed, and the feathers are—well— flawless, if I do say so myself."

Below me, the stadium roars—not with human voices, but with hoots, howls, chirps, roars, squeaks, and one extremely dramatic bray that rattles at least four of my feathers.

"Tonight," I say, pacing along my commentator's perch high above the field, "we welcome competitors from every continent on Earth. Seven continents. One massive showdown. Exactly zero participation trophies."

I pause.

"Medals, yes. Glory, yes. Eternal bragging rights? Absolutely. Participation trophies? Not on my watch."

Somewhere in the stands, a capybara squeaks in disappointment. Tough crowd.

Spotlights dim. A steady drumbeat rumbles across the arena like distant thunder.

"Here comes our first team!" I declare, pumping up the energy so high my own voice bounces back at me from the far seats.

The drums swell, and the announcer—me—booms again:

"Representing the hot savannas, deep jungles, and vast grasslands… Africa!"

They don't *walk* into the stadium.

They storm it.

Hooves thunder. Dust swirls. A line of zebras and antelopes trots forward in perfect rhythm, their stripes and coats flashing under the lights. Giraffes stride proudly behind them, necks rising high above the crowd. And leading the parade is a lion, mane glowing like wildfire, calm and powerful—while every other animal gives it a respectful amount of space.

"Africa wastes no time!" I shout. "Power! Speed! Style! And so far—so far!—no one has been eaten. A promising start."

The crowd erupts with roars, whistles, chirps, and one dramatic hiss I did *not* appreciate.

The drums fade. I clear my throat and boom again:

"Next... from forests, prairies, mountains, deserts, and icy tundra... North America!"

They enter like a marching band that replaced instruments with antlers.

A massive bison leads the group, hooves striking the track in steady beats. Wolves move behind it with proud, confident steps. Overhead, bald eagles swoop in synchronized arcs, their wings shimmering in the lights.

"Now *that* is entrance form!" I say. "Strong! Steady! Dramatic! And only slightly terrifying. North America is bringing the intensity early."

The bison snorts at me like it heard that. Hard to tell with bison.

"From the rainforests, rivers, soaring Andes, and wild plains... give it up for South America!"

Their entrance isn't a march.

It's a party.

Macaws explode into the air first, painting the stadium with flashes of red, blue, and gold. Tapirs trot in with howler monkeys perched on their backs, tails curled like question marks. Then the howlers throw their heads back and unleash calls that shake the rafters.

"My feathers!" I gasp, flattening them with one wing. "If you're listening from home, please adjust your volume. South America came here to make sure even the fossils in the museum heard them."

Spotlights shift. I deepen my voice.

"From ancient forests, rolling plains, and historic mountains... welcome Europe!"

Europe's entrance is calm, dignified, and—let's be honest—slightly dramatic.

Red deer glide forward in graceful lines. Behind them, brown bears lumber proudly, waving at the crowd with giant paws. Sleek lynx pad silently between them, perfect posture, perfect balance. Above, pigeons swoop into a flawless circle, then break into a burst that sparkles under the lights.

"Classic Europe," I narrate. "Elegant. Strategic. Those homing pigeons are so precise they could land on the same leaf twice. Not that I'm intimidated. (I am absolutely intimidated.)"

Lights sweep again.

"From the tallest peaks, deepest jungles, and far-reaching rivers... here comes Asia!"

Asia's entrance feels like a moving landscape.

Elephants lead the charge, trunks raised in greeting. Tigers walk behind them—quiet, confident, unmistakably in charge. Small monkeys chatter excitedly, hopping onto elephants' backs. A cloud of cranes glides overhead in absolute silence.

"Asia brings muscle, grace, and whisker power. And look at that teamwork! Monkey plus elephant equals the highest viewing platform in the stadium."

Next up, bright outback-orange lights flash.

"From deserts, reefs, rainforests, and the legendary Outback... welcome Australia!"

Australia bursts—literally—onto the field.

Kangaroos and wallabies bounce forward in long, graceful arcs. Koalas hold tight as they ride on their backs, clutching branches like VIP passengers. A sugar glider leaps from a platform, catching air and gliding in a smooth swoop above the group.

"Australia never walks," I say. "It *boings.* If I tried that, I'd sprain at least three feathers."

Finally, the lights drop to a cool, icy blue.

"And from the harshest winds on Earth... welcome Antarctica!"

Silence.

Then—FWIP!

A penguin slides belly-first out of the tunnel, gliding along a slick lane of ice. Behind it, a perfectly aligned column of penguins waddles in unison. A few seals flop along after them, flippers slapping the ground like applause.

"Now that is style," I whisper. "Penguins sliding like professional toboggans. I have *never* wanted to wear a tuxedo more."

Once the teams are lined up, the stadium falls still.

"Now," I boom, voice deep and dramatic, "for the moment we've all been waiting for: the lighting of the Olympic torch."

A single spotlight cuts through the dark.

"Our torchbearer," I explain, "is one of the rarest animals on Earth... a symbol of beauty, strength, and endangered species everywhere... the Amur leopard."

The crowd gasps as a sleek, golden leopard emerges—its winter coat thick and shimmering with pale silver-gold light. It carries the unlit torch gently in its jaws.

It walks the perimeter, every continent bowing slightly as it passes. Even the howler monkeys stay quiet. (A miracle.)

The leopard reaches the towering cauldron. With careful balance, it rises onto its hind legs. A spark ignites—

FWOOOSH.

The Olympic flame erupts, bright and powerful, lighting the entire stadium.

Emotion prickles through my feathers. I pretend it's just the heat.

"Ladies and gentle-animals," I say softly, "the Animal Olympics have officially begun."

Now, for the rules.

"Each event will award medals to our top three finalists," I explain. "A gold medal is worth three points, a silver medal is worth two points, and a bronze medal is worth one point."

"At the end of sixteen events," I continue, "one continent will be crowned Animal Olympics Champion of the World."

I glance across the field.

Continent	☆ Gold	🏅 Silver	🏅 Bronze	Total
Australia	0	0	0	0
Africa	0	0	0	0
Asia	0	0	0	0
Europe	0	0	0	0
N. America	0	0	0	0
S. America	0	0	0	0
Antarctica	0	0	0	0

Far away, I spot a cheetah stretching, a pronghorn flicking its ears, and—if I'm not mistaken—a coastal taipan practicing a smooth slither-warmup.

"Tomorrow," I say, lowering my voice, "we begin with the 100-Meter Dash. The fastest creatures on land."

I lean close to the mic.

"Do not blink. You might miss the whole thing."

The Animal Olympics are all fun and games—right up until someone forgets they're supposed to chase medals, not each other.

2 — THE 100-METER DASH

If you ever hear someone say, "The air was electric," let me assure you—they weren't here today. THIS air isn't electric.

It's *overcharged.*

You could fry an omelet on the tension alone. Not that I've tried. Yet.

"Welcome back, sports fans!" I announce, swooping onto my commentator perch. "Coach Talon here, and today's event is the one you've all been waiting for—the 100-Meter Dash! The fastest land animals on Earth are about to explode off the starting line faster than my Aunt Gloria when someone opens a bag of sunflower seeds."

Down on the track, the stadium lights brighten to a warm gold. Three lanes gleam across the ground—straight, perfect, and ready for speed.

The finalists step forward.

COACH TALON'S SCOUTING REPORT		
CHEETAH AFRICA	**PRONGHORN** NORTH AMERICA	**COASTAL TAIPAN** AUSTRALIA
SPEED: 60-70MPH **SPECIAL MOVE:** TURBO POUNCE **FUN FACT:** WHEN A CHEETAH SPRINTS, ITS TAIL HELPS IT TWIST AND TURN SO FAST YOU'D THINK IT'S STEERING WITH A GIANT FURRY BALANCE STICK.	**SPEED:** UP TO 55MPH **SPECIAL MOVE:** ENDURANCE OVERDRIVE **FUN FACT:** ITS POWERFUL HEART AND LUNGS LET IT KEEP HIGH SPEED FOR MILES. IF RUNNING LONG-DISTANCE WERE HOMEWORK, THE PRONGHORN WOULD FINISH BEFORE CLASS EVEN STARTED.	**SPEED:** 10-12 MPH IN SHORT BURSTS **SPECIAL MOVE:** ZIG ZAG STRIKE **FUN FACT:** FASTEST SLITHERER IN THE OUTBACK; IF SPAGHETTI COULD SPRINT, THIS IS EXACTLY WHAT IT WOULD LOOK LIKE

The crowd settles. Every continent's delegation leans forward—well, except Antarctica. The penguins lean *backward,* which is honestly impressive for a bird shaped like a sideways bowling pin.

I tap my clipboard.

"Let's break this down," I whisper dramatically. "The cheetah? Fastest sprinter alive. The pronghorn? The king of endurance speed. The coastal taipan? A surprisingly quick noodle of terror."

I pause.

"To be clear, I say 'noodle' respectfully."

Down on the field, the cheetah kneads the ground, muscles rippling under its coat. The pronghorn snorts and flicks its ears, already reading the wind. The taipan coils tightly, head raised, tongue flicking with confidence.

My feathers quiver.

"This... is going to be FAST."

A tortoise in a referee shirt carries a small flag to the track. It moves... intentionally. Slowly. Carefully.
Very, very carefully.

"Folks," I say, "our official starter is making the toughest walk of his career. Any slower and he'll be going backward in time."

When he finally reaches the side of the track, he raises one front leg.

The stadium holds its breath.

"Runners—ready!"

The cheetah crouches, tail straight.
The pronghorn leans forward.
The taipan coils in a perfect S, ready to launch.

I lean so close to the mic I bonk my beak against it.

"AND—"

FWIP! The tortoise waves the start flag.

The cheetah becomes a golden blur. One heartbeat and it's already halfway down the track. Dust explodes behind it. The stadium gasps so loudly I feel the air pressure change.

"Look at that acceleration!" I howl. "I felt a breeze and I'm not even on the ground!"

The pronghorn launches next—pure muscle, pure grace, sprinting with perfect form.

"North America isn't giving up!" I shout. "This is a pronghorn saying, 'Sure, you're fast, but can you do it for TWO MILES?'"

Finally, the taipan surges forward, body rippling like a living whip. Its slither is smooth, fast, and surprisingly straight. It must be saving that zig-zag for the right moment.

"Australia's taipan is holding strong!" I yell. "It may not match the mammals in speed, but look at that *technique!* That's a high-performance slither if I've ever seen one."

But the cheetah... The cheetah doesn't run. It detonates.

Ten strides. Twenty. Forty.

The finish line approaches like it's being pulled toward the cat. My feathers flatten from the wind the cheetah leaves behind.

"Ladies and gentle-animals—THIS IS HISTORY!"

"CHEETAH BREAKS THE TAPE!" I scream as Africa erupts in triumphant roars.

One second later—

"PRONGHORN CHARGES ACROSS!" North America stomps, howls, and cheers so loudly my perch shakes.

And only a few heartbeats behind—

"TAIPAN SLITHERS ACROSS THE LINE!"
Australia goes wild, a chorus of hops, squeaks, and enthusiastic boings.

I leap into the air, doing a small victory loop.

"Yes! YES! What a race! What a start to the Animal Olympics!"

Official Results

Gold — Africa (Cheetah)
Silver — North America (Pronghorn)
Bronze — Australia (Coastal Taipan)

Updated Standings After Event 1

Continent	☆ Gold	🏅 Silver	🥉 Bronze	Total
Australia	0	0	1	1
Africa	1	0	0	3
Asia	0	0	0	0
Europe	0	0	0	0
N. America	0	1	0	2
S. America	0	0	0	0
Antarctica	0	0	0	0

"If THAT was just Event One," I say, breathless though I haven't moved, "I hope you brought extra feathers, snacks, and emotional support. Tomorrow's event will be a whole different kind of wild."

I tap the mic.

"This is Coach Talon... and the Animal Olympics are officially off to a *flying* start."

Let's just hope everyone remembers tomorrow's competition is a sport—not a snack situation.

3 — THE HIGH JUMP

If you've ever wondered what tension looks like, imagine a kangaroo tightening its tail like a spring, an impala scrutinizing the sky, and a puma staring at a bar like it owes him lunch money.

That's what greets me when I land on my commentator's perch this morning.

"Welcome back, sports fans!" I say, tapping my headset to make sure it's on. "Coach Talon here, reporting live from Day Two of the Animal Olympics, and today's event is a certified feather-raiser: the High Jump!"

Below me, the stadium floor is covered in soft moss and sand—because safety first, even in extreme competition. A tall, sturdy bar stretches across two posts, steadily raised by a pair of meerkat officials wearing tiny referee vests.

COACH TALON'S SCOUTING REPORT		
IMPALA AFRICA	**RED KANGAROO** AUSTRALIA	**PUMA** SOUTH AMERICA
JUMP HEIGHT: UP TO 10 FEET VERTICALLY SPECIAL MOVE: ROCKET HOP FUN FACT: CAN LEAP IN ANY DIRECTION MID-RUN, LIKE IT'S PLAYING ITS OWN NEVER-ENDING GAME OF "FLOOR IS LAVA"	JUMP HEIGHT: UP TO 10 FEET VERTICALLY SPECIAL MOVE: POWER BOUNCE FUN FACT: ITS STRONG TAIL HELPS IT BALANCE AND PUSH OFF WHEN HOPPING — LIKE HAVING A BUILT-IN KICKSTAND FOR GIANT JUMPS.	JUMP HEIGHT: UP TO 18 FEET SPECIAL MOVE: SILENT SPRING FUN FACT: PUMAS JUMP SO QUIETLY AND SMOOTHLY THAT YOU DON'T EVEN SEE THE TAKEOFF...ONE SECOND IT'S HERE, THE NEXT IT'S ON A CLIFF PRETENDING IT'S BEEN THERE ALL DAY

"This event isn't about speed," I explain, puffing my chest. "It's about technique! Power! Leg springs so strong they could launch me to the moon! ...Not literally. I tried once. Didn't go great."

The crowd hushes. The finalists step forward.

The bar begins at a modest height — nothing these athletes can't handle, but perfect for warmups.

The kangaroo bounces lightly, testing the ground. The impala trembles with precision, wound like a living bowstring. The puma observes in silence, tail twitching like a ticking clock.

I clear my throat into the mic.

"In the High Jump, style matters. Height matters. And absolutely *not* knocking the bar down matters. Let's see which of our athletes reaches the clouds today!"

Round One

The meerkat referee squeaks a command I absolutely do not understand — but the kangaroo apparently speaks fluent meerkat.

He bounds forward—hop, hop—tail slamming down for a massive BOING! He arcs skyward and clears the bar with inches to spare.

"Australia starts strong!" I shout. "Look at that form! That tail is doing half the work!"

The crowd whoops in approval.

Next, the impala. No running start. No warmup hops. It simply *launches* upward like someone fired off a spring-loaded antelope.

"OH! Africa came to win today!" I cry, flapping my wings so fast I nearly lift off.

Then the puma trots up, calm and calculated. He crouches, pushes off, and glides over the bar with silent confidence.

All three finalists advance.

The meerkats squeak again and hoist the bar higher.

Round Two

Now the bar is high enough to make *me* uncomfortable — and I'm a bird.

The kangaroo inhales, bounces forward, and slams his tail down — THUNK — launching himself skyward like a marsupial cannonball.

Cleared.

The crowd erupts.

The impala steps back, circles once… twice… then springs upward with such precision it might as well be following an invisible elevator…that only goes UP.

Cleared.

"IMPRESSIVE!" I shout. "That antelope jumps higher than my enthusiasm at snack time!"

Finally, the puma.
Crouch. Leap. Glide —

DING.

His back paw grazes the bar.
It jiggles.
Wobbles.
Woooooobbles…

…and stays up.

I nearly swallow my whistle.

"OHH! South America survives by the power of whiskers and good fortune!"

Final Round

The meerkats raise the bar to an event-record height.

Now the real drama begins.

The kangaroo shakes out his arms, flicks his tail, and hops forward.

He crouches, thrusts upward —

And rises in a perfect arc, silhouetted against the sky.

CLEARED.

"Australia's kangaroo nails it!" I holler. "That landing! Ten out of ten! Someone give that tail a medal of its own!"

The crowd booms with excitement.

The stadium stills.

The impala steps back.
Takes one measured breath...

...and launches.

Straight up.
Effortless.
Elegant.

It floats over the bar like gravity decided to take a lunch break.

"Africa answers RIGHT BACK!" I roar. "What a leap! What a moment! Look at those magnificent hooves!"

The impala lands so lightly it barely disturbs the sand.

WOBBLE...WOBBLE...

"WAIT A MINUTE!" I declare, barely breathing as it becomes clear to the whole animal kingdom that the impala must have barely brushed the bar.

CRASH!

"That was closer than my encounter with that lion backstage this morning!"

Silence sweeps the stadium. Even the penguins freeze mid-waddle.

The puma crouches low, muscles tight, eyes locked on the bar.
He pushes off with everything he has —

But this time... he's just a hair short.

His shoulder brushes the bar and—

CLATTER!

Down it falls.

South America groans, but the puma bows his head with dignity.

"What an effort!" I call. "Our puma showed courage, class, and serious muscle. Today, though, the vertical crown belongs to our spring-loaded champion from Australia."

After a brief discussion, the meerkats award the runner-up tiebreaker to the Impala for unknown reasons (probably because they too are from Africa).

Official Results

Gold — Australia (Red Kangaroo)
Silver — Africa (Impala)
Bronze — South America (Puma)

Updated Standings After Event 2

Continent	☆ Gold	🥈 Silver	🥉 Bronze	Total
Australia	1	0	1	4
Africa	1	1	0	5
Asia	0	0	0	0
Europe	0	0	0	0
N. America	0	1	0	2
S. America	0	0	1	1
Antarctica	0	0	0	0

"SCOREBOARD AFTER EVENT 2," I declare, tapping my mic.

"And there you have it, folks! Australia's spring-powered superstar takes the gold, with Africa close behind — and kangaroos don't even wear heels!"

I chuckle proudly at my own joke, blissfully unaware that no one else does.

"Tomorrow, things get splashy — very splashy. Get your goggles ready! Coach Talon signing off!"

Let's just hope tomorrow's water event keeps things friendly...predators tend to swim faster when they're hungry.

4 — THE 50 METER SWIM

If you thought the stadium was loud during the High Jump, you should hear it today. The entire place sounds like a giant blender full of seawater, clapping seals, screeching gulls, and exactly one screaming otter who may or may not have invented its own cheer.

"Welcome back, speed fans!" I cry, beating my wings to hover above the aquatic arena. "Coach Talon here, reporting LIVE from the Animal Olympics' shimmering, splashing, absolutely soaking-wet Swimming Stadium!"

Today's event?

The 50-Meter Swimming Sprint.

A straight-line dash across a long, crystal-clear pool. The water glows under the sunlight, rippling like someone shook a giant jar of blue glitter until the whole pool sparkled.

"And folks," I add in a whisper loud enough to echo, "our swimmers today are FAST. Faster than fast. Faster than me when I hear someone open a bag of roasted pumpkin seeds."

The crowd roars as our finalists glide toward the starting blocks.

A giant splash pad surrounds the pool, because spectators on the front row have already accepted they're going home soaked. The meerkat referees stand at attention, wearing waterproof whistles.

Our finalists glide into position. I tap my clipboard.

"Let's talk technique," I narrate. "The sailfish is built for speed—its body is so streamlined it practically removes water in front of it. The dolphin? Power and intelligence combined. And the penguin? Compact, aerodynamic, and capable of turning tighter corners than my Aunt Gloria's shopping cart."

Coach Talon's Scouting Report		
Sailfish Europe	**Dolphin** North America	**Penguin** Antarctica
Speed: Up to 68 mph **Special Move:** Blade Dash **Fun Fact:** Can change the color of its skin during fast swims, almost like it's turning on "race mode"	**Speed:** Up to 25 mph **Special Move:** Power Glide **Fun Fact:** Communicates with clicks and whistles so well that it might be the only athlete who trash-talks in sonar.	**Speed:** 6-9 mph underwater **Special Move:** Torpedo Launch **Fun Fact:** Flaps its wings underwater like flippers, making it look like a tiny tuxedo torpedo with somewhere very important to be

I lower my voice dramatically.

"But today... no turning required. Just pure, blazing speed."

A walrus official swims to the center lane, raises two dripping flippers, and bellows something that sounds like "HHHHHRUUUAAHH!"

That means "racers ready," in case you don't speak Walrus.

The sailfish stills.

The dolphin lowers its body.

The penguin bobs once, twice... then strikes a determined pose that screams "I was born for this."

My feathers fluff in anticipation.

"AND—"

BWOOOOP!

They explode off the start.

The sailfish launches like a silver lightning bolt, slicing forward so fast the water barely realizes it's been disturbed. Its dorsal fin rises like a victory banner as it rockets ahead, leaving a rolling wake behind it that looks suspiciously like a tiny tsunami.

Right beside it, the dolphin powers forward with smooth, rhythmic tail strokes. Then — showoff that it is — it bursts upward into a perfect arc, splashing back down in its lane without losing an ounce of speed. The crowd gasps, cheers, claps, chirps — a whole orchestra of chaos cheering it on.

But here comes the penguin.

Small? Yes.

Outmatched in pure speed? Technically.

But determined? Absolutely.

The little bird kicks with rapid-fire flipper strokes, body straight as a torpedo, eyes locked on the finish line like it just insulted his dance moves. Underwater, it moves with a surprising swagger, weaving through the bubbles with tight, controlled bursts.

"Look at that FORM!" I shout. "The penguin may not win the sprint, but that underwater technique is GLORIOUS!"

All three racers churn forward — the sailfish still surging ahead in a blur, the dolphin sprinting with joyful power, the penguin pushing with every ounce of heart it has.

The pool becomes a frenzy of speed, spray, and pure aquatic determination.

The sailfish hits the far wall so fast I blink and nearly miss the moment. It taps the finish pad—

BEEP!

Gold for Europe!

A heartbeat later—

BEEP!

Silver for North America's dolphin!

And just a few seconds behind—

BEEP!

Bronze for the penguin!

The little diver pops out of the water, belly-slides across the mat, and bumps gently into the official's flippers.

The crowd explodes.

I nearly cartwheel in midair.

"WHAT A RACE! WHAT A SPLASH! WHAT A PENGUIN!"

Official Results

Gold — Europe (Sailfish)
Silver — North America (Dolphin)
Bronze — Antarctica (Penguin)

Updated Standings After Event 3

Continent	☆ Gold	🏅 Silver	🏅 Bronze	Total
Australia	1	0	1	4
Africa	1	1	0	5
Asia	0	0	0	0
Europe	1	0	0	3
N. America	0	2	0	4
S. America	0	0	1	1
Antarctica	0	0	1	1

"SCOREBOARD AFTER EVENT 3," I announce, fluffing my wings proudly.

"Ladies and gentle-animals, today's event was wetter than a seabird at a splash park! Europe surges back with a blazing sailfish victory, and Antarctica earns their first point thanks to one heroic penguin!"

I tap the mic.

"Tomorrow's competition takes us underground... literally. Get ready for dirt, determination, and some extremely enthusiastic digging claws."

"This is Coach Talon... and the Animal Olympics are just heating up — even in the water!"

And as our champions towel off, let's all hope tomorrow's underground athletes remember the rule of the day: compete with heart... not with hunger.

5 — THE BURROWING SPEED RACE

If you've ever tried digging in the ground with your bare wings, let me tell you—it ends poorly. And with dirt everywhere. And sometimes worms.

Fortunately, today's competitors are much better equipped than I am.

"Welcome back, tunnel enthusiasts!" I boom into my microphone as the crowd stomps, squeaks, chirps, and… somehow… vibrates with excitement. "Coach Talon here, coming to you live from the Animal Olympics' underground arena for the Burrowing Speed Race!"

The field looks like someone turned the stadium floor into a giant sandbox. Three starting holes have been dug at the north end of the arena. Three finish-mound targets sit 20 feet away.

And between them? Let's just say the meerkats got creative.

Roots. Pebbles. Hard-packed clay. Even a tiny underground flag marking the turnaround point.

"This event," I explain dramatically, "is a combo special: a down-and-back race AND an underground obstacle course. Dig down, reach the marker, turn around, and burst back up through the finish mound."

The stadium hushes as the finalists scurry forward.

Coach Talon's Scouting Report		
Wombat Australia	**Prairie Dog** North America	**Naked Mole Rat** Africa
Digging Speed: Slow, but powerful **Special Move:** Bulldozer Burst **Fun Fact:** Its backside is made of tough cartilage — great for blocking burrow entrances, and probably the only time having a "square butt" is a competitive advantage	**Digging Speed:** Up to 12 feet per hour in dense soil **Special Move:** Rapid Scratch **Fun Fact:** Lives in huge underground "towns" with rooms and tunnels so complex they're basically little neighborhoods with better zoning laws	**Digging Speed:** Unknown **Special Move:** Tooth Tiller **Fun Fact:** Because it uses teeth for digging, it can move each front tooth separately — yes, it basically has steering-wheel teeth

The prairie dog stands tall, scanning the course like a tiny general. The naked mole rat tests the soil with its front teeth, ready for business. The wombat... just stands there, calm and unbothered. Possibly thinking about snacks.

I lower my voice.

"This one is going to be TIGHT. Prairie dogs are fast. Naked mole rats are efficient. Wombats are slow but strong enough to move anything in their way. Let's DIG IN! Literally!"

A chipmunk referee raises a checkered flag nearly as big as itself.

"On your marks... get set..."

FWIP!

The flag drops.

They vanish underground in three completely different styles of chaos.

The prairie dog rockets downward first, disappearing so fast it's like someone dropped it through a secret trapdoor. A fountain of dirt explodes behind it, spraying the stadium floor like celebratory confetti.

Right beside its tunnel, the naked mole rat digs with smooth, rhythmic bites—its teeth working like a living jackhammer. Every movement is efficient, precise, unbelievably controlled. If digging were an art, this mole rat would have a gallery show.

And then there's the wombat.

Slow.

Steady.

Unstoppable.

It drops into its tunnel with a heavy THUD, scooping out massive chunks of earth with each swipe. Roots snap. Pebbles scatter. The ground rumbles with every deliberate push.

"Folks," I narrate breathlessly, "that wombat isn't fast—but it could dig a basement under your basement."

Soil erupts near the midpoint—
Prairie dog reaches the marker FIRST!

It spins underground and rockets back toward the finish, claws scratching like tiny turbo-engines.

North America goes wild.

But right behind—

A perfectly carved tunnel appears at the marker as the naked mole rat pops up, taps the flag with its nose, and disappears again with zero wasted motion.

"Africa is RIGHT BEHIND!" I yell. "That mole rat knows its geometry!"

Then—

A deep rumble.

A tremor.

A furry earthquake.

The wombat bursts up beside the marker, sniffs once, then bulldozes straight back underground in the direction of the finish mound.

Australia loses its mind.

The stadium floor starts popping — full underground whack-a-mole chaos.

The prairie dog bursts upward—
...but a foot too far left.

"Oh NO! North America took a wrong turn!" I squawk. "That's what happens when you dig blind at top speed!"

It chirps in frustration and dives back down.

Next, the mole rat pushes upward—
RIGHT under the correct mound.

But the top is thick, packed tight. It scratches frantically, teeth working overtime.

"Africa's mole rat is PERFECTLY placed!" I shout. "But that final burst is tough!"

Then—

A low rumble.

Dust rising.

A wobble under my perch.

Suddenly—

KABOOM!

The wombat erupts through the finish mound like a dirt volcano, blasting the top clean open.

"AUSTRALIA BURSTS THROUGH!" I scream. "THE WOMBAT'S POWER PAYS OFF!"

Half a second later, the mole rat breaks free— Second place!

Two heartbeats later, the prairie dog pops out— Third!

Official Results

Gold — Australia (Wombat)
Silver — Africa (Naked Mole Rat)
Bronze — North America (Prairie Dog)

Updated Standings After Event 4

Continent	☆ Gold	🏅 Silver	🏅 Bronze	Total
Australia	2	0	1	7
Africa	1	2	0	7
Asia	0	0	0	0
Europe	1	0	0	3
N. America	0	2	1	5
S. America	0	0	1	1
Antarctica	0	0	1	1

"SCOREBOARD AFTER EVENT 4," I announce.

"Ladies and gentle-animals, we have a TIE for first place overall! Australia and Africa both have seven points—and we're only four events in!"

I flap my wings dramatically.

"This race for global glory is tighter than a squirrel squeezing into a bird feeder. Not that I've seen that. Recently."

I try to wink. Birds can't wink. I blink aggressively instead.

"Tomorrow, prepare for MUSCLE MADNESS. The Strength Lift will shake this stadium. I'm Coach Talon... signing off before someone burrows under my chair!"

Let's hope tomorrow's Strength Lift involves lifting weights... not lifting each other like snacks.

6 — THE STRENGTH LIFT

If you thought the digging event was intense, welcome to the Strength Arena—where even the *ground* looks nervous.

The stadium floor is covered in logs, stones, massive boulders, weighted platforms, and one suspiciously shiny metal slab the meerkats clearly found behind the stadium and decided, "Yes. This is heavy enough."

"Good day, muscle marvels!" I shout, pumping my wings as the crowd erupts. "Coach Talon reporting LIVE from the Animal Olympics' Strength Lift—the event where power meets pride and gravity usually loses!"

Dust swirls. Something roars. Something else roars louder. Even the penguins look intimidated, which is rare—they normally only fear running out of fish.

Our three finalists lumber into the spotlight, and suddenly I feel very, *very* small.

COACH TALON'S SCOUTING REPORT		
GORILLA AFRICA	**BROWN BEAR** EUROPE	**ASIAN ELEPHANT** ASIA
MAX LIFT: OVER 1000 LBS IN SHORT BURSTS **SPECIAL MOVE:** POWER PRESS **FUN FACT:** HAS SUCH STRONG ARMS IT CAN CLIMB, SWING, AND LIFT LIKE IT'S TRAINING FOR EVERY EVENT AT ONCE — THE ULTIMATE CROSS-FIT CONTESTANT	**MAX LIFT:** 700 LBS **SPECIAL MOVE:** BOULDER ROLL **FUN FACT:** HAS A BITE STRONG ENOUGH TO CRUSH BOWLING BALLS... THANKFULLY IT PREFERS BERRIES, FISH, AND NOT SPORTING EQUIPMENT OR BALD EAGLES	**MAX LIFT:** 600+ LBS USING TRUNK **SPECIAL MOVE:** TRUNK HOIST **FUN FACT:** AN ELEPHANT'S TRUNK IS SO POWERFUL IT CAN LIFT HUGE WEIGHTS — YET GENTLE ENOUGH TO SCRATCH AN ITCH WITHOUT BONKING ITSELF.

The Strength Lift isn't just one test—it's a gauntlet.

First comes the Boulder Hoist, where our competitors have to lift a stone so massive the meerkats had to paint arrows on it just to decide which side was "up."

Next is the Log Press, a thick, heavy tree trunk waiting to be thrust overhead with sheer muscle and willpower.

And finally, the grand finale: the Slab Push, a weighted platform that must be shoved all the way across the finish line like it insulted somebody's ancestors.

"Three challenges," I announce, fluffing my feathers for dramatic effect. "One winner. And a whole lot of roaring. Let's begin before the bear eats the equipment."

A giant boulder sits center stage. The competitors take their positions for the first challenge, muscles tensed, each one ready to make geology nervous.

The brown bear goes first, gripping the rock with a determined huff. It lifts—

RIIIIISE—
chest height—
wobbles—
and drops it with a dusty THUD.

"Respectable attempt from Europe!" I shout. "For a moment I thought that boulder was about to file a complaint."

Silence falls as the gorilla steps up. It plants its feet. Grips tight. Lowers its massive shoulders.

Then—
With a thunderous rumble—
HEAVES IT SKYWARD!

Chest-height. Higher… Higher…

And then—ROOOOAR! The gorilla holds it overhead for a full three seconds.

The stadium explodes.

"Africa showing SERIOUS strength!" I yell. "That boulder went higher than my expectations—and I set them PRETTY HIGH!"

Then the elephant approaches. Calm. Focused. Unbothered.

It wraps its trunk around the stone and lifts it casually—
CASUALLY!
—as if it were picking up a coconut someone dropped at a picnic.

The crowd stares. I nearly faint.

"Asia… wins round one!" I shout. "That wasn't lifting—that was levitating with style!"

A thick tree trunk rests on supports. The air hums with anticipation as the competitors approach the second challenge.

The bear goes first again, rising to full height and pressing the log upward with a guttural roar. It locks its elbows—
one second—two—
and drops it with a THUMP.

"Well done, Europe!" I cheer.

The gorilla steps up next, crouches, grips, and rockets the log overhead like it's made of cotton fluff.

Five seconds.
Six.
Seven.

"WHAT A HOLD!" I scream. "Hire that gorilla for all your furniture-moving needs!"

The crowd loses it.

Then the elephant approaches the log... and hesitates.

It wraps the trunk around it, lifts—
but the size throws off the leverage.

It still raises the log, but only to shoulder height.

"A reminder, folks!" I call out. "In strength events, SIZE isn't everything—unless we're talking about the log, which is apparently *too* big to trunk-lift!"

Round two goes to the gorilla.

A giant weighted slab sits waiting like a stubborn boulder that refuses to roll. The most difficult challenge of all, number three, begins.

The bear digs in, pushes—
and slides the slab five feet.

Respectable.

The gorilla steps up next, breathes deep, and—

SHOVE!

The slab rockets forward eight feet, spraying sand everywhere.

"Africa is ON FIRE today!" I shout, clinging to my perch.

Last comes the elephant.

It lowers its head.
Plants its massive feet.
Braces.

And—

BOOOOM!

One single push sends the slab sliding ALL THE WAY across the finish line.

The stadium goes silent—
then explodes louder than a volcano full of cheering meerkats.

I drop my whistle from shock.

"ASIA DOMINATES ROUND THREE!"

Official Results

Gold — Asia (Asian Elephant)
Silver — Africa (Gorilla)
Bronze — Europe (Brown Bear)

Updated Standings After Event 5

Continent	☆ Gold	🏅 Silver	🏅 Bronze	Total
Australia	2	0	1	7
Africa	1	3	0	9
Asia	1	0	0	3
Europe	1	0	1	4
N. America	0	2	1	5
S. America	0	0	1	1
Antarctica	0	0	1	1

"SCOREBOARD AFTER EVENT 5!" I shout over the roaring crowd. "Asia storms onto the board with a massive win! Africa stays in the lead, and Europe muscles up another point!"

I tap my whistle.

Amazing strength today—though I kept one eye on the exits. When predators get fired up, sometimes the snacks... I mean spectators... get nervous.

"But don't stretch those wings—or legs—too soon. Tomorrow's event isn't about power... it's about stamina. Grit. Determination. And the ability to keep going long after your feathers are begging you to stop."

I lean close to the mic, whispering dramatically:

"Get ready for the Endurance Marathon. The longest, toughest test of will in the entire Olympics."

7 — THE ENDURANCE MARATHON

Some events make the crowd roar.
Some events make the ground shake.
This event makes ME tired just *looking* at it.

"Welcome back, stamina superfans!" I cry, landing on my high perch with a puff of feathers. "Coach Talon here, reporting LIVE from the Animal Olympics' Endurance Marathon—where our competitors will run farther than I fly on Thanksgiving."

The racecourse winds through the stadium, dips into the forest path, loops around the river, and returns along a long straightaway marked with giant flags. As for the distance? The meerkats didn't bother measuring it. They just wrote "A LOT" on the scoreboard.

Today isn't about speed.
It's about grit.
Willpower.
Leg power.
And in one case—hooved, unstoppable determination.

COACH TALON'S SCOUTING REPORT		
WILDEBEEST AFRICA	**CARIBOU** NORTH AMERICA	**IBEX** EUROPE
STAMINA: RUNS HUNDREDS OF MILES IN MIGRATION **SPECIAL MOVE:** ENDLESS TROT **FUN FACT:** TRAVELS IN MASSIVE HERDS THAT CAN RUN TOGETHER FOR DAYS — BASICALLY THE BIGGEST CROSS-COUNTRY TEAM ON EARTH	**STAMINA:** ALL AROUND LONG DISTANCE STAMINA **SPECIAL MOVE:** SNOW GLIDE **FUN FACT:** THEIR HOOVES CLICK WHEN THEY WALK AND RUN, SO THE ENTIRE HERD SOUNDS LIKE A GIANT RUNNING CLUB WEARING TAP SHOES	**STAMINA:** HILL RUNNING ENDURANCE **SPECIAL MOVE:** CLIFF CLIMBER **FUN FACT:** HAS HOOVES WITH A HARD OUTSIDE EDGE AND A SOFT, GRIPPY CENTER — BASICALLY NATURE'S VERSION OF CLIMBING SHOES

The crowd quiets as the finalists step forward.

A soft breeze moves across the arena. The penguins fall silent. The elephants wave their trunks solemnly. Somewhere, a monkey drops its snack in anticipation.

"This," I whisper, "is a battle of wills. A showdown of stamina. A test of who can defeat the greatest enemy of all—time."

The wildebeest paws the ground with confidence.

The caribou snorts, antlers gleaming.
The ibex stretches one hind leg like it's about to win an elegant mountain yoga contest.

A meerkat referee climbs onto a stump and raises a tiny flag.

"Runners... ready..."

FWIP!

They're off.

A cloud of dust rises as the three endurance champions surge forward together.

The wildebeest settles instantly into its famous tireless trot—smooth, efficient, as steady as a metronome.
"Look at that FORM!" I shout. "That's a migration machine right there!"

The caribou runs close behind, hooves tapping the ground in a rhythmic pattern that sounds like winter wind over snow.

"This is North America's bread and butter! Or snow and moss, technically!"

The ibex stays perfectly in stride, legs springing with mountain-born precision. It looks almost insultingly relaxed.

"Europe is HOLDING STRONG! Someone put a mountain out here—they'd actually speed up!"

The runners disappear briefly into the forest path, their hoofbeats fading into distant echoes.

"This part tests patience," I narrate. "You can't sprint a marathon. Well, *I* can't sprint anything over ten seconds, but that's not the point."

They emerge still tightly grouped—
Wildebeest in front,
Caribou leaning into a steady surge,
Ibex close behind but unmistakably unfazed.

The course bends beside a shimmering river. The wildebeest inches forward with a subtle burst. The caribou answers with a powerful, even push. The ibex keeps perfect rhythm, adjusting effortlessly to shifting terrain.

"This race is TOO CLOSE!" I croak. "Someone bring me a glass of water—my feathers are sweating!"

The final turn brings them back into the stadium, where the crowd erupts with a roar of anticipation. The long straightaway stretches ahead like a test of destiny itself.

The wildebeest lengthens its stride, muscles rippling with migration-level grit. The caribou digs deep, every step fueled by legendary endurance. The ibex drives forward, determined to turn mountain power into miracle speed.

"THIS IS IT!" I scream. "The final showdown of stamina!"

They thunder down the straightaway— the wildebeest holding the lead,

the caribou gaining steadily,
the ibex pushing with every ounce of strength.

The stadium rises to its feet.

Thirty yards.
Twenty.
Ten.

The wildebeest unleashes one last surge—

AND CROSSES THE LINE FIRST!

Africa erupts in celebration.

Seconds later, the caribou charges through the finish for silver, followed closely by the ibex, cheered on by a corner of mountain goats ringing tiny bells.

I collapse dramatically onto my perch.

"WHAT. A. RACE."

Official Results

Gold — Africa (Wildebeest)
Silver — North America (Caribou)
Bronze — Europe (Ibex)

Updated Standings After Event 6

Continent	☆ Gold	🥈 Silver	🥉 Bronze	Total
Australia	2	0	1	7
Africa	2	3	0	12
Asia	1	0	0	3
Europe	1	0	2	5
N. America	0	3	1	7
S. America	0	0	1	1
Antarctica	0	0	1	1

"Ladies and gentle-animals," I announce, catching my breath despite doing zero running, "Africa extends its lead with a marathon masterclass! North America ties Australia for second place, and Europe adds another point to stay in the game."

Somewhere during that final sprint, I swear I saw a look that said, 'If this weren't a race... you'd

be lunch.' Friendly competition can get...
competitive.

I flap my wings.

"But rest those legs, because tomorrow we take to the SKY! That's right—speed, stamina, and strength step aside. It's time for feathers, flair, and high-flying spectacle."

I puff my chest proudly.

"Get ready for the Aerial Acrobatics Challenge—the event I personally *would have dominated* if they hadn't banned coaches from competing. A tragic loss for the sport."

8 — AERIAL ACROBATICS

Some events make the ground shake.
Others make the water churn.
This one makes the sky jealous.

"Welcome back, sky-gazers!" I shout, landing on my perch with a dramatic flap. "Coach Talon here, reporting LIVE from the most glamorous, neck-craning, eye-widening event of the Olympics—the Aerial Acrobatics Freestyle! Thirty seconds. One sky. Three incredible birds. And absolutely NO safety nets!"

Today's setup is simple:

"Each bird gets thirty seconds to impress our judges with creativity, skill, daring maneuvers, and absolute mastery of the sky. No hoops. No obstacles. Just pure airborne brilliance."

I turn to the judging table.

"And speaking of judgment... allow me to introduce our panel! First, the Great Horned Owl—silent, serious, and already analyzing someone's wing angles. Next to him, the macaw—dripping in beads, color, and sass. And finally, the mallard, who takes landing technique more seriously than taxes."

The macaw waves proudly. The owl stares intensely. The mallard adjusts his posture like he's preparing to grade a runway show.

COACH TALON'S SCOUTING REPORT		
BARN SWALLOW Europe	**HARPY EAGLE** South America	**PEREGRINE FALCON** Africa
FLYING STYLE: SMOOTH AND AGILE **SPECIAL MOVE:** QUICK WEAVE **FUN FACT:** EATS INSECTS WHILE FLYING — LITERALLY SNACKS MID-FLIGHT, TURNING EVERY RACE INTO AN ALL-YOU-CAN-EAT BUFFET	**FLYING STYLE:** POWERFUL AND COMMANDING **SPECIAL MOVE:** SILENT SWEEP **FUN FACT:** TALONS ARE AS BIG AS A GRIZZLY BEAR, NOT SOMEONE YOU SHOULD TRY AND STEAL A SNACK FROM	**FLYING STYLE:** PURE VELOCITY **SPECIAL MOVE:** SUPERSONIC DIVE **FUN FACT:** FASTEST ANIMALS ON EARTH, MAKE CHEETAHS SAY: "OKAY, THAT'S JUST SHOWING OFF"

The barn swallow steps onto the launch perch, chest puffed out proudly. It gives a polite little bow—adorable—then springs into the sky with a burst of speed.

What happens next is... pure art.

The swallow loops. It zips. It spirals. It draws shapes in the air so fast I give up guessing what the shapes are. For a moment, it slips between two

drifting clouds and emerges soaring backward.
BACKWARD.

The crowd squeals.

"That's not flying—that's sky calligraphy!" I
shout.

The swallow finishes with a tiny flutter-spin and
lands so lightly the perch doesn't even wiggle. The
mallard's jaw drops. The macaw claps wildly,
beads jangling. The owl blinks once—high praise
from an owl.

The owl lifts a card: 9.
The macaw flashes a bold, sparkly 10—with a tiny
drawn heart.
The duck raises a 10 with a proud nod.

Europe is on the board and the stadium is
roaring.

Next comes the harpy eagle, stepping forward
like royalty. The crowd quiets instantly. I sit up
straighter without meaning to.

With one powerful beat of its wings—

WHOOMPH!

The harpy rises in a slow, spiraling climb. Every
movement is deliberate. Smooth. Controlled.

Halfway up, it freezes mid-air—just holding, perfectly still—before tipping into a long, dramatic glide that sweeps right over the judges' table.

Feathers ripple. Hats fly off. The macaw screams in delight.

Then the harpy pulls into a slow-motion barrel roll, wings stretched to their full, enormous span. It glides home and lands with a thump so confident I'm tempted to salute.

The owl studies the landing, then raises an 8, looking impressed.
The macaw flashes a bright, colorful 9, tossing confetti that I'm 90% sure isn't allowed.
The duck hesitates... then pushes up a perfect 10.

"MAGNIFICENT!" I cry. "Someone paint that bird on a mountain!"

Silence.
A hush spreads across the crowd.

The falcon steps up, lowering into a sprinter's crouch—yes, birds can do that—and then launches into the sky so fast the air makes a sound I'm not sure is legal.

It disappears into the clouds. Completely. Totally.

One second...
Two...
Three...

Then—
FWIP!

It drops out of the sky like a feathered meteor.
The stadium gasps as it pulls up inches above the ground and slashes into a sideways spin so tight / get dizzy.

The falcon climbs again, performs a backward loop, folds its wings for a heartbeat, then snaps them open in a dazzling flourish before drifting down onto the perch with laser-perfect accuracy.

The owl raises a 10, calm but stunned.
The macaw lifts a 10 decorated with a little star and sparkles.
The duck slaps down a 10 so fast he nearly pecks the card.

The crowd detonates.

"That was ILLEGAL LEVEL AMAZING!" I scream. "Someone check the rulebook—did we allow teleportation?!"

Official Results

Gold — Asia (Peregrine Falcon)
Silver — Europe (Barn Swallow)
Bronze — South America (Harpy Eagle)

Updated Standings After Event 7

Continent	☆ Gold	🏅 Silver	🏅 Bronze	Total
Australia	2	0	1	7
Africa	2	3	0	12
Asia	2	0	0	6
Europe	1	1	2	7
N. America	0	3	1	7
S. America	0	0	2	2
Antarctica	0	0	1	1

The standings tighten—so do my feathers.

"SKY MAGIC!" I yell, nearly losing my headset. "Asia rockets upward! Europe, North America, and Australia are all TIED behind Africa, and South America shows off enough drama to star in its own nature documentary!"

I applaud the athleticism—and quietly appreciate that no one mistook another competitor for lunch.

I tap my mic.

"But fold those wings, friends—because tomorrow's event is a sharp turn from aerial elegance. Literally sharp. VERY sharp. The kind of sharp that makes me glad I have a beak guard at home."

I lean in dramatically.

"Next up is Precision Pecking—a contest of accuracy, focus, and poking things with STYLE."

9 — PRECISION PECKING

There are three kinds of silence.

Regular silence.

Awkward silence.

And the kind of silence that happens right before someone pecks something extremely important.

This is the third kind.

"Welcome back, accuracy addicts!" I whisper (dramatically, of course) into the mic. "Coach Talon reporting LIVE from the Precision Pecking Arena—where focus is king, nerves are tested, and beaks are SHARP."

The field is set with three tall posts, each topped with a circular wooden target—concentric rings, bright paint, freshly sanded faces ready for battle.

The rules? Simple.

One bird.

One beak.

One shot.

Punch a hole clean through the center.

But today feels different.
Today feels... heavy.

This is the MIDPOINT event.
Halfway through the Olympics.
A turning point.

And every continent knows it.

Africa leads—but barely.
Europe, North America, and Australia are locked

in a tight cluster.

Asia is gaining.

South America and Antarctica are desperate to get on the board.

The tension is so thick you could spread it on toast.

COACH TALON'S SCOUTING REPORT		
PENGUIN ANTARCTICA	**WOODPECKER** NORTH AMERICA	**RED-CROWNED CRANE** ASIA
STYLE: QUICK, ACCURATE POKES **SPECIAL MOVE:** ICE PECK POP **FUN FACT:** WALKS AROUND IN A TUXEDO AND STILL MANAGES TO LOOK SERIOUS WHILE PECKING — TRULY COMMITTED TO FORMAL COMPETITION	**STYLE:** RAPID-FIRE PECKING WITH PINPOINT ACCURACY **SPECIAL MOVE:** DRUM ROLL **FUN FACT:** HAS A BUILT-IN SHOCK ABSORBER IN ITS SKULL SO IT DOESN'T RATTLE ITS OWN BRAIN — NATURE'S BEST HELMET	**STYLE:** SPEAR-LIKE PRECISION **SPECIAL MOVE:** LIGHTNING JAB **FUN FACT:** FAMOUS FOR GRACEFUL DANCES, SO EVEN ITS PECKS LOOK LIKE PART OF A FANCY PERFORMANCE ROUTINE

The stadium falls silent.

Three birds.

Three posts.

Three targets thick enough to take dozens of hits.

"This event," I whisper, "is simple: keep pecking until your beak breaks all the way through (or until your beak breaks). No stopping. No hesitating. First bird to punch daylight wins."

My feathers tremble.

This is going to get LOUD.

A meerkat referee raises the flag.

FWIP!

The flag drops—

They explode forward.

The woodpecker reaches its post first and unleashes a lightning storm of blows:

TAP-TAP-TAP-TAP-TAP-TAP-TAP!

A blur of feathers and fury. Splinters fly. The board trembles like it's begging for mercy.

"OH BOY!" I howl. "That's a skull BUILT for impact!"

The crane arrives a breath later, planting its stance with deadly calm. It strikes in slow, devastating jabs:

THUNK... THUNK... THUNK...

Each blow lands deeper than the woodpecker's—less frantic, more surgical.

"Asia is playing the long game!" I cry. "Precision over chaos! Strategy over speed!"

Then waddles the penguin—adorably determined—and throws itself into the board with all the courage of a bird who has zero business being this brave.

BONK! BONK! BONK!

Cute?
Yes.
Ineffective? Shockingly no.
Determined? Absolutely.

"GIVE IT EVERYTHING, LITTLE BUDDY!" I scream, already losing my professional neutrality.

Wood chips rain down like snow.

The woodpecker's frantic tapping has carved out a crater, deep and messy.
The crane's deliberate jabs have formed a clean

tunnel, narrow but dangerously deep.
The penguin is... making a dent. A noble dent. The world's bravest dent.

Antarctica chants in unison. It's weirdly inspiring.

"Three totally different strategies!" I shout. "Science teachers everywhere are LOVING THIS!"

Then—

A sharp, echoing CRACK!

The entire arena freezes.

Both the woodpecker's AND the crane's target faces fracture, spiderwebbing across the wood.

"It's ANYONE'S race!" I yell. "NORTH AMERICA'S SPEED vs. ASIA'S POWER!"

The crane shifts its stance—focus razor-sharp—and lands a brutal, deep jab.

KRRRCK!
A chunk of wood falls away.

Asia explodes in cheers.

But the woodpecker responds with a burst so fast the air seems to buzz:

TAP-TAP-TAP-TAP-TAP-TAP—CRACK!

A slab of wood bursts off the target.
Light flickers through the crater.

"It's about to BREAK!" I cry.

"Kid's, if you are watching at home, don't try this!" I shout as the pecking nears the end.

The woodpecker's crater widens—daylight shining through like a tiny sunrise. The crane's tunnel deepens—just a breath from punching out the back. The penguin keeps pecking with heroic stubbornness.

"COME ON, PENGUIN!" I shout, fully unhinged.

The entire stadium joins:

PECK! PECK! PECK! PECK!

Wood shakes.
Dust rises.
Splinters fall like confetti at a birthday party for lumberjacks.

Then—

CRRRRAAAAAAACK!

The woodpecker's beak blasts through the board, sending shards flying like wooden fireworks.

"BREAKTHROUGH! NORTH AMERICA WINS!" I scream, nearly fainting.

Seconds later—

KR-SHNK!

The crane pierces through with a perfect, elegant circle of daylight.

Asia erupts.

And finally—

TIK—TIK—TIK—CRACK!

A tiny piece falls from the penguin's board.
Light shines through.
Antarctica loses its collective mind.

Penguins are sliding everywhere.
One judge starts crying.
And—fine—I tear up a little too.

Official Results

Gold — North America (Woodpecker)
Silver — Asia (Red-Crowned Crane)
Bronze — Antarctica (Gentoo Penguin)

Updated Standings After Event 8

Continent	☆ Gold	🏅 Silver	🏅 Bronze	Total
Australia	2	0	1	7
Africa	2	3	0	12
Asia	2	1	0	8
Europe	1	1	2	7
N. America	1	3	1	10
S. America	0	0	2	2
Antarctica	0	0	2	2

Friendly competition or not, something about sharp beaks and rising pressure makes instincts twitch.

"WHAT A SHOWDOWN!" I shout, voice cracking like a snapped twig. "North America SMASHES their way into second place! Asia drills through the competition! And ANTARCTICA—oh sweet, flippered glory—finally breaks onto the scoreboard!"

I press a wing to my chest.

"The momentum has SHIFTED, folks. These Olympics are officially wide open!"

I lean toward the mic, voice dropping low for maximum drama.

"But don't cool those feathers just yet. Tomorrow's goal? Fly the farthest—without actually flying."

I wink.

"Some animals are going to soar. Others are going to belly-flop."

I grin.

"Get ready for the Long Jump. The runway is set, the sand pit is fluffed, and I've already seen three contestants practicing their 'please don't land on your face' drills."

10 — THE LONG JUMP

Some events are all muscle. Some are all heart. But this one?

This one is all legs—beautiful, spring-loaded, science-defying legs.

"Welcome back, leap legends!" I shout as I flutter onto my commentary perch, narrowly avoiding a meerkat raking the sand. "Coach Talon reporting LIVE from the Animal Olympics Long Jump—the event where gravity takes a lunch break!"

The runway is smooth.
The sand pit is pristine.
The tension is sky-high.

Because today, we've got one jumper from three continents—each a world-class leaper in their own *very* different way. The crowd vibrates like the stadium itself just took a deep breath.

COACH TALON'S SCOUTING REPORT		
KLIPSPRINGER AFRICA	**KANGAROO RAT** AUSTRALIA	**LYNX** NORTH AMERICA
JUMP LENGTH: 25 FEET **SPECIAL MOVE:** PEBBLE HOP **FUN FACT:** STANDS ON THE VERY TIPS OF ITS HOOVES, GIVING IT UNBELIEVABLE BALANCE — BASICALLY THE BALLERINA OF MOUNTAIN GOATS	**JUMP LENGTH:** 7 TO 9 FEET **SPECIAL MOVE:** PREDATOR ESCAPE MEGA HOP **FUN FACT:** CAN JUMP SO QUICKLY IT LOOKS LIKE IT TELEPORTS — ONE SECOND YOU SEE IT, NEXT SECOND IT'S SOMEWHERE ENTIRELY DIFFERENT AND PROBABLY GIGGLING	**JUMP LENGTH:** 20 FEET **SPECIAL MOVE:** SILENT POUNCE **FUN FACT:** THOSE GIANT, SNOWSHOE-LIKE PAWS HELP IT STAY STEADY AND JUMP FAR — GREAT FOR RUNNING ON SNOW, TERRIBLE FOR FINDING SHOES THAT FIT

The meerkat officials smooth the sand, check the measuring sticks, and nod at each other like they're defusing a bomb.

I clear my throat.

"Classic long jump rules today! One runway. One leap. Farthest distance wins. Style points don't count—though I personally appreciate them."

A tortoise referee raises his tiny green flag. The crowd hushes.

Let the jumping begin.

The klipspringer steps onto the runway first, light on its hooves like it barely weighs more than a feather. It lowers its body... pauses... then SPRINGS forward—

BOING!

It arcs high—higher—then forward, sailing through the air like a four-legged rocket scientist reinventing physics. It lands softly in the sand, perfectly upright, not a wobble in sight.

The meerkats race over with measuring sticks.

7.4 meters!

"AFRICA OPENS HUGE!" I shout. "That is ROCK-SHATTERING range!"

The stadium explodes with cheers.

Next up is the kangaroo rat.

It hops to the start line, tail flicking nervously. It's small. It's adorable. It looks like it should be competing in a tiny-leaps competition at recess—yet here it is, facing giants.

It wiggles.
It crouches.
It hops once...

And then FWIP!—it BLASTS off the runway.

The tiny superhero sails shockingly far, ears flapping, eyes wide with midair commitment. It lands with a gentle puff of sand.

The meerkats huddle.

2.8 meters!

"WHAT A JUMP FOR ITS SIZE!" I cry. "Australia shows heart, courage, and aerodynamics that defy its snack-sized body!"

The crowd loses its mind.

Finally, the lynx steps up.
The stadium goes quiet.

Muscles coiled.
Eyes locked on the landing pit like it owes him money.
Three slow steps...
A crouch...
A deep inhale—

WHOOMPH!

The lynx launches in a silent, devastating leap—like a predator teleporting across a meadow. It soars, lands in a graceful skid, and rises proudly.

The meerkats measure.

6.1 meters!

"NORTH AMERICA TAKES SECOND!" I squawk. "A POUNCE FOR THE AGES!"

The stadium roars.

Official Results

Gold — Africa (Klipspringer)
Silver — North America (Lynx)
Bronze — Australia (Kangaroo Rat)

Updated Standings After Event 9

Continent	☆ Gold	🥈 Silver	🥉 Bronze	Total
Australia	2	0	2	8
Africa	3	3	0	15
Asia	2	1	0	8
Europe	1	1	2	7
N. America	1	4	1	12
S. America	0	0	2	2
Antarctica	0	0	2	2

Africa widens the gap. North America not far behind.

"WHAT A LEAP-FEST!" I shout, feathers on end. "Africa springs ahead! North America pounces into second!! And Australia proves once again that being small just means you break the laws of physics harder!"

85

Watching a predator land that close to smaller competitors always makes me double-check the rulebook... and the exits.

I tap my mic.

"But tomorrow... ohhhh tomorrow... things get FAST. And chaotic. And entirely dependent on not dropping stuff."

I grin with dangerous enthusiasm.

"Get ready for the Relay Race — the first full-team event of the Olympics! Speed, passing skills, and absolute mayhem await!"

11 — THE TEAM RELAY RACE

Running events are fast.
Running events are fun.
But TEAM running events?

Those are absolute chaos with a stopwatch.

"Welcome back, speed fans!" I shout, swooping above the oval track like a feathery drone. "Coach Talon here, reporting LIVE from the very first Team Relay Race in Animal Olympics history! And I'm already sweating—and I haven't even done anything!"

Three teams step onto the track, each radiating confidence—or something trying very hard to *look* like confidence.

The reindeer team from Europe prances into lane one, antlers high and hooves clicking proudly.

Asia's saiga antelopes slip into lane two, noses puffing like they're preheating for turbo mode.

And North America's coyotes take lane three, wearing expressions that say, "We've already planned six different ways to win this."

Each runner carries a tiny branch-shaped baton—yes, branch-shaped. Don't ask. Meerkats were involved.

The crowd buzzes.
This isn't just an event.
This is a MILESTONE in Olympic teamwork.

COACH TALON'S SCOUTING REPORT		
SAIGA ANTELOPE TEAM ASIA	**COYOTE TEAM** NORTH AMERICA	**REINDEER TEAM** EUROPE
STRENGTH: SMOOTH, STEADY, AND FAST **SPECIAL MOVE:** GLIDE RUN **FUN FACT:** THAT BIG BOUNCY NOSE? WORKS LIKE A NATURAL AIR FILTER... AND PROBABLY WINS "MOST SURPRISING SNOUT IN TRACK & FIELD"	**STRENGTH:** ADAPTABLE, STRATEGIC RUNNERS **SPECIAL MOVE:** TRICKSTER BURST **FUN FACT:** SMART ENOUGH TO CHANGE STRATEGIES MID-RUN — THE COYOTE MIGHT BE THE ONLY ATHLETE HOLDING A PLAYBOOK.	**STRENGTH:** WINTER ENDURANCE AND SURPRISING SPEED **SPECIAL MOVE:** HOLIDAY HUSTLE **FUN FACT:** CAN OUTRUN MOST PREDATORS WHEN MOTIVATED... OR WHEN CHRISTMAS IS COMING.

The meerkats place the starting batons neatly on the ground.

I hover above the stadium.

"Each team will run four legs around the track," I explain. "Fastest team wins. Clean baton handoff required. No tripping, no biting, and DEFINITELY no howling during the handoff. Yes, I'm looking at you, coyotes."

The tortoise referee raises the flag...

FWIP!

The race begins.

Asia surges ahead immediately.

The saiga antelope in lane two blasts off like it has jet engines attached to its hooves.

North America keeps pace.

The first coyote starts strong, staying within a stride of Asia.

Europe... oh boy.

The reindeer team starts... fine... at a respectable winter-trot pace.

But on a racetrack?
They look like they're warming up for December.

"They're pacing themselves," I say diplomatically. "Either that or Santa forgot to feed them espresso today."

The crowd laughs.
Europe groans.

Asia's second saiga antelope takes the baton with a flawless transfer—smooth as melted butter—and rockets forward even faster.

North America's handoff is decent, keeping them in the race.

Europe's handoff?

WHUMP.

The baton drops.

The reindeer freezes in horror.

My heart almost stops.

"Oh NO!" I shriek. "EUROPE DROPS THE BATON! That's the kind of mistake that lands you on Santa's naughty list!"

The crowd gasps.

A meerkat races in, signaling they can keep going—
but the reindeer team is now dead last.

"Well... on the bright side," I improvise, "at least they're used to pulling SLEIGHS uphill. This is nothing compared to Christmas Eve cardio!"

The crowd laughs despite the tension.

The reindeer pick up the baton and sprint harder.
MUCH harder.

Asia still leads—but the pacesetter saiga is showing signs of fatigue.

North America is steady, holding second.

Europe?
Europe is FURIOUS.

Their third reindeer SNATCHES the baton and bolts forward with holiday-level determination.

"This reindeer is running like it's late delivering gifts!" I holler. "SANTA would be proud of this hustle!"

The crowd roars.

Reindeer closes on the coyote.
Then passes the coyote.
Then closes in on Asia—

The stadium goes WILD.

From last place…
to second…

The comeback is happening.

The final three runners line up.

A blazing-fast saiga for Asia.
A coyote with fierce eyes for North America.
A surprisingly intense reindeer for Europe.

Asia gets the baton first and tears off with a massive lead.

North America follows.

Europe gets the baton last—
but the reindeer launches forward like a festive missile.

"LOOK AT HIM GO!" I scream. "He's flying! He's soaring! He's—wait, is he allowed to fly? No? Okay, good, he's just REALLY fast."

The reindeer gains on the coyote.
Passes the coyote.
The stadium erupts.

Now it's just Europe vs. Asia.

The saiga still holds a lead—
but the reindeer is CLOSING the gap.

Twenty meters left.

Fifteen.

Ten.

Five.

The reindeer lowers its head—

AND SURGES AHEAD IN THE LAST THREE STEPS!

The finish line explodes in cheers.

Europe wins
BY HALF A NOSE.

Reindeer and their noses! Yes, that was one last reindeer Christmas joke...

Official Results

Gold — Europe (Reindeer Team)
Silver — Asia (Saiga Antelope Team)
Bronze — North America (Coyote Team)

Updated Standings After Event 10

Continent	☆ Gold	🏅 Silver	🏅 Bronze	Total
Australia	2	0	2	8
Africa	3	3	0	15
Asia	2	2	0	10
Europe	2	1	2	10
N. America	1	4	2	13
S. America	0	0	2	2
Antarctica	0	0	2	2

The entire standings tighten AGAIN.

This Olympics has become a pressure cooker so hot you could fry an egg on my feathers.

"WHAT A RACE!" I shout, puffing up like popcorn. Asia rockets into contention! North America battles to the very end! And that reindeer team just completed a comeback even Santa would call a Christmas MIRACLE!"

The crowd is quiet except for the crickets. I guess that was one too many Christmas jokes.

I tap my mic.

"And tomorrow... oh, tomorrow... things get PHYSICAL. No finesse. No flair. Just raw strength versus strength."

I lower my voice.

"It's time for the Tug-of-War. Bring your muscles. Bring your grip. Bring your chiropractor."

12 — TUG-OF-WAR

There are moments in sports that require elegance.
Moments that require strategy.
Moments that require brains.

This event requires none of those things.

"WELCOME BACK, MUSCLE MANIACS!" I screech as I flap above the field. "Coach Talon here, reporting LIVE from the Tug-of-War arena—where strength is king, teamwork is everything, and the rope is older than I am!"

A giant braided rope stretches across the field, thick enough to tow a mountain. Painted in the middle, bright as a warning sign, is the Victory Line—aka what I lovingly call "The Border of Existential Defeat."

Three teams stomp onto the grass, radiating so much raw power I reflexively tighten my feathers:

Africa's Rhino Team.
South America's Giant Otter Team.
Antarctica's Elephant Seal Team. (Yes, Antarctica is using seals again. Yes, the seals insisted.)

Why these three?
Because these continents brought the most ridiculously strong creatures they could find. The kind that could pull houses, logs, boulders, or—apparently—each other.

The crowd vibrates with anticipation.

"Ohhh, this is going to be JUICY," I whisper, rubbing my wings together.

COACH TALON'S SCOUTING REPORT		
RHINO TEAM AFRICA	**GIANT OTTER TEAM** SOUTH AMERICA	**ELEPHANT SEAL TEAM** ANTARCTICA
STRENGTH: CAN PUSH THOUSANDS OF POUNDS WITH SHOULDERS **SPECIAL MOVE:** THE BULLDOZER LEAN **FUN FACT:** ITS HORN IS MADE OF THE SAME STUFF AS YOUR HAIR — JUST, YOU KNOW... WAY STRONGER AND FAR LESS STYLISH	**STRENGTH:** TEAM COORDINATION AND SURPRISING POWER **SPECIAL MOVE:** THE SYNCHRONIZED TUG **FUN FACT:** LIVES IN FAMILY GROUPS SO WELL ORGANIZED THEY'RE NICKNAMED "OTTER SQUADS," AND TRUST ME, YOU DO NOT WANT TO FACE AN OTTER SQUAD IN TUG OF WAR	**STRENGTH:** MASSIVE BODY WEIGHT **SPECIAL MOVE:** THE GLACIER SLIDE PULL **FUN FACT:** CAN WEIGH OVER 8,000 POUNDS — WHICH MEANS WHEN IT SAYS IT'S NOT MOVING, NOTHING ON EARTH IS CHANGING ITS MIND

The stadium falls silent as the teams take their places—not at opposite ends of a rope, but each at a different corner of a giant rope triangle.

Yes. A literal triangle.

The meerkats tied it themselves.
They are extremely proud of this.

In the center stands a tall pole with a bright red ribbon tied around it. Whichever team pulls the ribbon closest to their corner wins.

I stretch my wings and try to sound scholarly.

"Three teams. Three corners. One rope. Zero sanity. This is Triangle Tug-of-War—patented, trademarked, and invented approximately ten minutes ago."

The crowd LOVES it.

The tortoise referee raises his green flag—

FWIP!

And the match begins.

The rhinos slam backward first, digging trenches in the grass with sheer power. Their corner of the triangle lurches back instantly, the ribbon jerking toward Africa.

"Africa TAKES THE EARLY LEAD!" I roar. "Those rhinos are pulling like they're trying to rearrange the continent!"

But the otters aren't here to be spectators.

They chant together—
"PULL! PULL! PULL!"—
and yank in perfect rhythm, bodies moving with

synchronized precision that puts dance troupes to shame. The rope trembles as their teamwork counters the rhinos' brute force. Slowly, the ribbon creeps back toward center.

"Incredible coordination!" I shout. "Otters don't just swim together—they PRANK together, COOK together, and apparently WIN SPORTS together!"

Then Antarctica engages.

The elephant seals brace... slide... wiggle... something. Whatever technique they're attempting, it's enthusiastic enough to count.

They lean back with trembling bellies and flippers digging into the turf—

And unbelievably, the rope shifts an inch toward them.

"THE SEALS ARE IN THIS!" I scream. "THEY ARE USING SHEER BODY MASS AND UNAPOLOGETIC CONFIDENCE!"

The crowd explodes with joy.

Now all three teams dig in.

Rhinos grunt and claw at the ground. Otters shout their rhythmic battle cry. Elephant seals vibrate with terrifying determination.

Dust rises.

Grass tears.

The rope triangle trembles under the strain.

Then it happens.

A rhino slips—just a tiny misstep—but enough
to break Africa's flawless formation.

The ribbon lunges toward South America.

"AFRICA STUMBLES! OTTERS SURGE AHEAD!" I
shriek. My voice cracks; I pretend it's a dramatic
choice.

Sensing opportunity, the seals give a mighty,
synchronized shove—

FWOOOMP!

The entire rope triangle tilts alarmingly toward
Antarctica's corner.

THE CROWD GOES NUCLEAR.

ANTARCTICA—
THE UNDERDOG OF THE CENTURY—
is inches from taking the lead.

The seals bark triumphantly.

Now it's all three teams at maximum effort.

Watching predators and prey pull on the same rope without pulling each other apart restores a little faith in sports.

The rhinos are snorting, stamping, roaring. The otters are pulling in tight, perfect formation. And the seals... they are sliding backward like living avalanche chunks.

The ribbon shakes violently—
drifts toward the otters—
rhinos counter—
seals counter THAT—
otters scream their rally cry:

"PULL! PULL! PULL!"

The triangle jolts.

The pole wobbles.

And finally—

With a massive coordinated yank—

SOUTH AMERICA WINS!

The red ribbon rockets toward their corner.

The whistle blows.

South America ERUPTS.

Otters slide across the grass in chaotic victory laps. One even starts crowd surfing. Africa bows their heads. Antarctica belly flops in celebration.

And me?

I'm screaming my feathers off.

Official Results

Gold — South America (Giant Otter Team)
Silver — Antarctica (Elephant Seal Team)
Bronze — Africa (Rhino Team)

Updated Standings After Event 11

Continent	☆ Gold	🏅 Silver	🏅 Bronze	Total
Australia	2	0	2	8
Africa	3	3	1	16
Asia	2	2	0	10
Europe	2	1	2	10
N. America	1	4	2	13
S. America	1	0	2	5
Antarctica	0	1	2	4

For the FIRST time...

The bottom two continents climb.
The battlefield shifts.
The pressure skyrockets.

"WHAT A MATCH!" I yell, feathers exploding off my wings. "South America shocks the WORLD! Antarctica SLIPS into silver! And Africa squeezes out a point that keeps their lead JUST barely breathing!"

I clutch the mic dramatically.

"But tomorrow... we leave the grass behind. We leave the dirt behind. We leave sanity behind."

I grin.

"Because next up is the Ice Slide Race—a slippery, chaotic, chilly mess of speed and survival. Bring your scarves, folks."

13 — THE ICE SLIDE RACE

Some events are chilly.
Some events are dangerous.
And some events are so chilly *and* so dangerous
that the waiver you sign is longer than the
rulebook.

"Welcome back, frost-fans!" I shout, gliding in a
nervous circle above the wildest, slipperiest track
ever created by meerkat engineers. "Coach Talon
here, reporting LIVE from the Ice Slide Race—a
twisting, turning, spiraling slip-and-scream festival
carved out of solid ice!"

Below me, the track gleams like a frozen serpent. It starts with a steep plunge, whips into a vicious banked turn, drops into a corkscrew spiral, shoots across a sideways-tilted wall, and finally launches racers off a snow ramp toward the finish.

"Simple rules," I announce. "Stay on the ice. Slide as fast as you can. Try not to scream louder than your coach."

COACH TALON'S SCOUTING REPORT		
SEA OTTER NORTH AMERICA	**ARCTIC FOX** EUROPE	**PENGUIN** ANTARCTICA
STYLE: SLEEK, STREAMLINED BODY AND POWERFUL TAIL FOR STEERING **SPECIAL MOVE:** SPIN-AND-GLIDE SLIDE **FUN FACT:** ITS FUR IS SO THICK IT TRAPS AIR BUBBLES, MAKING THE OTTER EXTRA BUOYANT AND EXTRA WARM — BASICALLY THE FLUFFIEST WETSUIT IN THE RACE	**STYLE:** SHARP CLAWS AND NIMBLE PAWS FOR ICY TERRAIN **SPECIAL MOVE:** SNOW DIVE **FUN FACT:** ITS PAWS ARE COVERED IN THICK FUR, GIVING IT NATURAL SNOW BOOTS — GREAT FOR GRIP, AND GREAT FOR STYLE POINTS	**STYLE:** BORN BELLY-SLIDER WITH PERFECT BALANCE AND LOW CENTER OF GRAVITY **SPECIAL MOVE:** TURBO TUMMY SLIDE **FUN FACT:** USES SLIDING TO TRAVEL FASTER THAN WALKING — IF THERE WERE HALLWAYS IN ANTARCTICA, PENGUINS WOULD DEFINITELY SLIDE THROUGH THEM

At the top of the starting ramp, our three competitors shuffle forward—each one looking very prepared… or pretending.

The meerkats finish buffing the track with little rags until the ice shines like glass. One meerkat licks it, gets stuck for thirty seconds, and is freed only after several teammates tug on his tail.

The tortoise referee trudges forward with a frosty blue flag. He lifts it dramatically.

"Here we go," I whisper. "One slide. One winner. Three opportunities for me to faint."

FWIP!

The flag drops.

The race begins.

The penguin reacts instantly—
dives onto its belly—
and ROCKETS down the ramp like a sleek, feathery missile.

The sea otter launches right behind, flopping onto its stomach and yelling something that sounds exactly like "WHOOO-HOOOO!"

The arctic fox attempts to sprint... misjudges the ice... and immediately spins into a fluffy white blur.

"They're off!" I shout. "Antarctica takes the lead! North America close behind! And Europe... well... Europe is redefining gravity!"

The steep drop accelerates all three racers. Ice chips spray out behind them like glittery fireworks.

A brutal right-hand curve appears.

The penguin leans into it, belly hugging the ice with absolute mastery. It glides around the bend like it's auditioning for the world's coldest roller coaster.

The otter slams into the wall—
BONK!
bounces off—
corrects—
hits the wall again—
and somehow slingshots forward even faster.

"North America turns the wall into a BOOST PAD!" I scream. "Genius! Chaos! Chaotic genius!"

The fox skids into the turn sideways, claws scraping frantically. Snow flies. The fox yelps—but holds the curve with impressive stubbornness.

Then comes the corkscrew spiral: a frozen tornado engineered for maximum drama.

The penguin dives in first, body perfectly aligned, gliding through the spiral like it's been training for this moment since hatch day.

The otter enters next—
spins once,
spins twice,
spins THREE times—
on purpose.

...maybe.

"SEA OTTER IS HAVING THE TIME OF ITS LIFE!" I yell. "I'm not sure it remembers this is a race!"

The arctic fox hits the spiral and spins so fast it becomes a white blur of panic, paws, and regret— but somehow pops out the other side still upright.

"Europe is defying physics," I whisper. "Or begging them for mercy."

Now the track tilts into a sideways wall—a steep, angled sheet of ice that requires either incredible skill... or a total disregard for self-preservation.

The penguin glides across it effortlessly. Born ready.

The otter fishtails wildly, tail snapping for balance, almost losing it—and then pulling off a miraculous recovery.

The fox sees no other option, flops onto its side, and lets momentum take over. Fur bristling. Eyes huge. Pride gone.

The crowd can't even pick a favorite anymore—they're just screaming joyfully at EVERYTHING.

All three racers blast out of the tilt and into the final straightaway, a downhill stretch ending in a snow ramp.

The penguin leads.
The otter is gaining.
The fox is hanging on through sheer stubborn willpower.

They hit the snow ramp—

WHOOSH—WHOOSH—WHOOSH!

The penguin goes airborne—sleek, steady, majestic.
The otter spins mid-air like a furry helicopter but somehow sticks the landing perfectly.
The fox performs an unintentional, terrifying midair flip that is definitely NOT in the manual.

They skid toward the finish—

The otter inches closer—
The fox digs deep—
But the penguin—
KING OF ALL THINGS ICY—

CROSSES THE LINE FIRST.

"PENGUIN WINS!" I roar. "ANTARCTICA CLAIMS
THE ICE CROWN!"

The crowd erupts.
Snow showers through the air.
Someone throws a fish.
The penguin catches it without even slowing down.

Official Results

Gold: Antarctica — Penguin
Silver: North America — Sea Otter
Bronze: Europe — Arctic Fox

Updated Standings After Event 12

Continent	☆ Gold	🏅 Silver	🏅 Bronze	Total
Australia	2	0	2	8
Africa	3	3	1	16
Asia	2	2	0	10
Europe	2	1	3	11
N. America	1	5	2	15
S. America	1	0	2	5
Antarctica	1	1	2	7

Africa still leads—
but North America is right behind,
and everyone else is closing in.

The entire Olympics feels like a rubber band pulled tight.

"WHAT A RACE!" I yell, skidding slightly on my icy perch. "Antarctica BLASTS back into the fight! North America hangs on to second! Europe spins, slips, crashes—and STILL takes a medal!"

I gesture dramatically toward the towering rock-and-ice climbing wall rising on the far side of the stadium.

"But tomorrow... we stop sliding and start climbing. No more help from gravity. Just claws, hooves, paws, and pure grit."

I lower my voice.

"Next up is the Climbing Competition—where up is hard, down is scary, and falling is... highly discouraged."

14 — THE CLIMBING COMPETITION

There are simple events.

There are complicated events.

And then there are events specifically designed to make me say, "Absolutely not, I'm not climbing that."

"Welcome back, altitude enthusiasts!" I call as I flap in a very wobbly orbit around a skyscraper-sized climbing wall. "Coach Talon here, reporting LIVE from the Rock Climbing Competition—where our athletes will challenge gravity, endurance, mental strength, and apparently a family of mountain goats who REFUSE to vacate the upper ledges."

The cliff rises in jagged, uneven slabs—some steep, some vertical, and one section I'm convinced is upside-down. The meerkats have planted tiny victory flags at the summit, which somehow makes the whole death-defying structure look festive.

At the base of the wall stand today's climbers:

Africa's Leopard, muscles coiled, tail twitching, confidence shimmering like a golden warning sign. Asia's Sun Bear, heavy-clawed and sturdy, gripping a practice log like it insulted its family. South America's Sloth, blinking slowly, stretching lazily, and yawning directly into the camera.

I lower my mic.

"Yes, folks—the sloth is here. Yes, it climbs. And yes… somehow… it believes it is winning today."

The crowd laughs.

They shouldn't.

Not yet.

COACH TALON'S SCOUTING REPORT		
LEOPARD AFRICA	**SUN BEAR** ASIA	**SLOTH** SOUTH AMERICA
CLIMBING STYLE: EXPLOSIVE, POWERFUL CLIMBER WITH BALANCE **SPECIAL MOVE:** SILENT SCRAMBLE **FUN FACT:** STRONG ENOUGH TO HAUL ITS FOOD UP INTO TREES — IMAGINE DOING PULL-UPS WHILE CARRYING DINNER	**CLIMBING STYLE:** STRONG, FOCUSED, AND SUPER GRIPPY **SPECIAL MOVE:** CLAW GRIP CLIMB **FUN FACT:** HAS A CRAZY-LONG TONGUE (UP TO 10 INCHES!) FOR REACHING INSECTS — NOT USEFUL FOR CLIMBING, BUT EXCELLENT FOR WINNING "WEIRDEST TALENT" BACKSTAGE	**CLIMBING STYLE:** SLOW, STEADY, UPSIDE-DOWN CLIMBER **SPECIAL MOVE:** SLOW-MO PULL-UP **FUN FACT:** ONLY COMES DOWN FROM TREES ABOUT ONCE A WEEK — TALK ABOUT CONSERVING ENERGY BETWEEN COMPETITIONS.

The meerkats scurry around polishing the base of the wall and giving thumbs-up to absolutely no one. The tortoise official climbs onto his podium (a process requiring three assistants) and finally raises the flag.

"Climbers," I announce, "first to the top claims glory. Second earns bragging rights. Third receives a very polite encouragement clap."

FWIP!

The flag drops. The race begins.

The leopard shoots upward like someone fired it out of a tree cannon. In seconds, it's leaping between ledges, claws digging deep, hind legs launching it upward in perfect, explosive bursts.

"Africa OPENS LIKE A ROCKET!" I yell, flapping so hard I drift backward. "That's not climbing—that's vertical sprinting!"

Below, the sun bear begins its ascent with calm determination. Movement by movement, claw by claw, it climbs with slow, deliberate rhythm. Every grip is solid. Every pull is powerful.

"Asia is climbing SMART," I say. "Not fast—but flawless. And sometimes flawless wins."

And then...

There is the sloth.

The sloth reaches toward the wall...
pauses...
scratches its cheek...
yawns...
and then grabs the next hold with serene confidence.

The crowd chuckles, but I lean into my mic dramatically.

"Mock not the sloth," I warn, "for it possesses the sacred power of Doing One Thing Very Slowly But Very Well."

And sure enough, the sloth begins climbing—slowly, yes, but absolutely climbing—grip steady, technique perfect, attitude relaxed.

Halfway up, the climbers reach the event's deadliest challenge: *the overhang.*

The leopard reaches it first.

It launches upward—
misjudges the angle—
slips—
catches itself by a *single claw*—
swings its entire body like a gymnast—
then hurls itself up and over the ledge.

The stadium explodes.

Moments later, the sun bear arrives. It grips the underside, fights for purchase, slips backward in a terrifying lurch—then unleashes a roar and muscles itself over the ledge with raw, undeniable power.

Asia stays alive.

And then there is the sloth.

It reaches the overhang...
pauses...
and simply *hangs there*.

Not struggling.
Not panicking.
Just chilling like it's sunbathing on a hammock.

Because sloths — unlike every other animal on Earth — are BUILT for dangling.

The audience goes silent.

Then, with slow-motion elegance, the sloth curls upward, hooks its limbs, and slides over the ledge in one fluid, jaw-dropping motion.

The stadium GASPS.

Wait...
Is the sloth...
GOOD at this?!

As the summit nears, the leopard begins to slow. The explosive bursts that gave it the early lead finally take their toll. Its breaths come heavy. Its strides shorter.

The sun bear keeps climbing with steady, grinding determination.

And below them both, unbelievably, the sloth continues climbing at its EXACT SAME SPEED— slow, steady, tireless.

I clutch my headset.

"SOUTH AMERICA IS BACK IN THIS!" I scream. "THE SLOTH IS DOING THE THING! THE ACTUAL THING!"

The leopard lunges for the final ledge—
slips—
recovers—
but loses precious momentum.

The sun bear tries to push harder—
but the nearly vertical slope slows it to a crawl.

And then the sloth arrives.

Calm.
Precise.
Unbothered by gravity or common sense.

It grips.
It climbs.
It rises.

Slowly...
smoothly...
inevitably...

The sloth pulls ahead.

The entire stadium rises as one roaring wave.

The sloth reaches the summit—
extends one arm with dramatic, slow-motion
flair—

AND TOUCHES THE FLAG FIRST.

South America wins the climbing event.

THE CROWD GOES FERAL.

Otters are fainting.
Penguins are sliding wildly.
Even the tortoise referee looks impressed—and he
hasn't changed his expression since 1984.

Official Results

Gold — South America (Sloth)
Silver — Asia (Sun Bear)
Bronze — Africa (Leopard)

Updated Standings After Event 13

Continent	☆ Gold	🥈 Silver	🥉 Bronze	Total
Australia	2	0	2	8
Africa	3	3	2	17
Asia	2	3	0	12
Europe	2	1	3	11
N. America	1	5	2	15
S. America	2	0	2	8
Antarctica	1	1	2	7

South America surges into contention.
Asia slowly climbs within striking distance of the lead. Africa remains on top, but barely.

"WHAT! A! SHOCKER!" I shout, feathers rattling. "South America pulls off the UPSET OF THE CENTURY! Asia stays hot on North America's tail! Africa nabs a critical point! And the SLOTH—THE SLOTH—has redefined athletic possibility!"

I slap a wing to my headset as the sloth slow-dances in the background.

"But tomorrow... things get LOUD."

I grin mischievously.

"Prepare for the Loudest Call Competition—an event so noisy I brought backup earmuffs, a backup mic, and a backup set of feathers."

15 — THE LOUDEST CALL

There are loud sounds in the world.

Thunder.

Volcanoes.

My cousin Barry snoring after chili night.

But NOTHING—and I mean NOTHING—comes close to today's event.

"Welcome back, brave eardrum volunteers!" I shout from my perch beside the biggest sound-measuring tower I've ever seen. "Coach Talon here, reporting LIVE from the Loudest Call Competition—where the only things louder than the contestants are the regrets of the officials who agreed to judge them!"

The arena is PACKED. Every continent feels the pressure—because with only three events left, the standings are tighter than penguins sharing a blanket. Every point matters. Every sound matters. Every decision matters.

And today's competitors?

They are legends.

Standing in the center field, preparing their vocal cords, are a howler monkey from South America, an Elk from North America, and my worst nightmare from Africa.

COACH TALON'S SCOUTING REPORT		
HOWLER MONKEY SOUTH AMERICA	**ELK** NORTH AMERICA	**LION** AFRICA
CALL STYLE: DEEP, BOOMING ROARS THAT ECHO FOR MILES **SPECIAL MOVE:** ECHO BLAST **FUN FACT:** HAS A HUGE THROAT POUCH THAT WORKS LIKE A NATURAL MEGAPHONE — THE MONKEY VERSION OF A STADIUM SPEAKER SYSTEM	**CALL STYLE:** HIGH, EERIE BUGLES **SPECIAL MOVE:** WILD BUGLE **FUN FACT:** ELK BUGLES CAN BOUNCE THROUGH FORESTS AND VALLEYS, MAKING IT SOUND LIKE THEY'RE EVERYWHERE AT ONCE… EVEN WHEN THEY'RE JUST SHOWING OFF.	**CALL STYLE:** DEEP, THUNDEROUS ROAR **SPECIAL MOVE:** THUNDER ROAR **FUN FACT:** A LION'S ROAR CAN BE HEARD UP TO FIVE MILES AWAY—BASICALLY NATURE'S WAY OF SAYING, 'THIS TERRITORY IS TAKEN.

I swallow so hard my headset squeaks.

"Fun fact," I whisper, "lions can roar loud enough to shake your soul. Funner fact: I am VERY SMALL AND VERY ROARABLE."

The lion glances up at me.
I almost fall off my perch.

Meerkats roll out a towering decibel meter—blinking lights, spinning dials, and a giant microphone shaped like an open ear. It looks like something a mad scientist would build on accident.

126

The tortoise referee steps forward, clears his throat with the volume of a polite cough, and announces:

"One call each. Highest decibel reading wins."

Simple.
Terrifying.
Scientific.

He raises the flag.

FWIP!

The Loudest Call Competition begins.

The elk steps forward first, lowering its head with regal confidence. It inhales deeply, filling its lungs like it's about to summon ancient mountain spirits—

BUUUGGGLLLLEEEEEEE!!

The call sweeps across the arena, haunting and powerful.

The meter jumps:
87 dB.

The crowd applauds—part admiration, part "Ow, my sinuses."

"Strong opening!" I shout. "Somewhere in the Rockies, a hiker just dropped their granola bar and doesn't know why!"

My feathers stand straight up.

Then the lion saunters out.

It plants its paws.
Lifts its magnificent head.

And unleashes—

RROOOOOOOOOAAAARRRRRR!!!

The sound SLAMS into the meter like a sonic meteor.
My cardboard shield rips in half.
A meerkat is blown backward into a cotton candy machine.
The decibel meter flails, lights blinking wildly.

112 dB.

"TERRIFYING PERFORMANCE FROM AFRICA!" I scream, mostly shouting because I can't hear anything anymore. "THAT ROAR MADE MY SOUL LEAVE AND COME BACK!"

The stadium goes wild.

Then the howler monkey steps up—
swaggering—
throat pouch inflating—
attitude at maximum.

It inhales.

And unleashes—

HOOOOOOOOOWWWWWWWLLLLLLLLLL!!!!!

The arena shakes.
The rafters tremble.
The decibel tower tilts like it's reconsidering its life choices.

The meter spikes...
flickers...
tries to escape...
and lands on:

136 dB.

The highest reading of the day.
By FAR.

"BY THE GREAT TROPICAL RAINFORESTS!" I shriek, diving behind my perch. "THE HOWLER MONKEY JUST BROKE THE DECIBEL SCALE—AND POSSIBLY MY LEFT EAR!"

The crowd erupts into total, joyous chaos.

South America jumps for joy.

The monkey howls again—mercifully quieter.

Africa nods with regal approval. I think the lion sees me so I start chanting: "AFRICA! AFRICA!"

Official Results

Gold — South America (Howler Monkey)
Silver — Africa (Lion)
Bronze — North America (Elk)

Updated Standings After Event 14

Continent	☆ Gold	🥈 Silver	🥉 Bronze	Total
Australia	2	0	2	8
Africa	3	4	2	19
Asia	2	3	0	12
Europe	2	1	3	11
N. America	1	5	3	16
S. America	3	0	2	11
Antarctica	1	1	2	7

"TENSION!" I shriek, feathers still vibrating. "Africa clings to a razor-thin lead! North America and Asia are right behind! Europe and South

America are lurking with potential! And there are only TWO events left!"

I gesture dramatically toward the field, where meerkats are building an obstacle course of tunnels, swinging ropes, seesaws, hurdles, spinning wheels, teetering ramps, and—oh no—a mud pit angled at a concerning degree.

"Prepare yourselves," I warn.

"Tomorrow is the Obstacle Course—a race so chaotic, so unpredictable, so BONKERS that even the meerkats wear helmets."

16 — THE OBSTACLE COURSE

There are races.
There are endurance contests.
And then there is the Obstacle Course—
 an event handcrafted by meerkats who clearly enjoy watching other animals struggle for their lives.

"Welcome back, chaos enthusiasts!" I shout from the announcer's booth as a rotating fan whips my feathers into dramatic disarray. "Coach Talon here, reporting LIVE from an obstacle course so twisted, so devious, so COMPLETELY BONKERS that it should come with a warning label, two waivers, and emotional support popcorn."

Below me stretches a labyrinth of tunnels, ramps, tire tubes, rope nets, seesaws, spinning platforms, and a mud pit so questionable it should probably be declared a biohazard.

The competitors line up.

Cute? Yes.
Friendly? Absolutely.
About to battle for continental glory? OH, VERY MUCH YES.

COACH TALON'S SCOUTING REPORT		
WALLABY Australia	**RACCOON** North America	**HEDGEHOG** Europe
AGILITY STYLE: EXPLOSIVE VERTICAL LEAPS	**AGILITY STYLE:** ADAPTIVE, PROBLEM SOLVER	**AGILITY STYLE:** LOW TO GROUND GRIT AND BALANCE
SPECIAL MOVE: BOUNCE DASH	**SPECIAL MOVE:** MASKED MANEUVER	**SPECIAL MOVE:** ROLL 'N' RUN
FUN FACT: COMMUNICATES WITH FOOT THUMPS ON THE GROUND — SORT OF LIKE TEXTING, BUT LOUDER AND DOESN'T REQUIRE A CELLULAR PLAN	**FUN FACT:** ITS FRONT PAWS ARE SO SENSITIVE IT CAN "SEE" WITH TOUCH — GREAT FOR OBSTACLE COURSES, BAD NEWS FOR ANYONE GUARDING SNACKS	**FUN FACT:** COVERED IN THOUSANDS OF TINY SPINES USED FOR PROTECTION — NOT IDEAL FOR HUGS, BUT EXCELLENT FOR KEEPING THE COMPETITION FROM BUMPING TOO CLOSE

Only two events remain.

Every movement counts.

Every slip could lose a championship.

Every cheer rattles the stadium.

The tortoise referee raises the flag.

"Brace yourselves," I whisper dramatically.

FWIP!

They're off.

The wallaby BLASTS forward so explosively the air makes a WHOOOMPH sound. It clears the first hurdle in one bound. Then two. Then the entire row in a single, majestic, physics-defying leap.

"AUSTRALIA IS BREAKING THE LAWS OF REALITY!" I squawk. "That wallaby isn't running— IT'S SKY-HOPPING!"

The stadium erupts as the wallaby ricochets between ramps and platforms, springing with ballet-like grace. It dives into the rope maze—

BOING!

—and springs out the other side completely untangled.

"ILLEGAL LEVELS OF BOUNCE!" I scream, unable to contain myself. "I NEED A RULING ON THIS. POSSIBLY FROM A SCIENTIST."

The wallaby is unstoppable.

North America's raccoon studies the obstacles first—eyes narrowed, tail twitching, brain calculating like a tiny, adorable supercomputer.

Then it moves.

It darts under hurdles, skirts the mud pit, swings through the rope net like a pirate captain, and scurries across a balance beam with its tail held out like the world's cutest counterweight.

"BEHOLD! CRAFTINESS AT ITS PEAK!" I shout. "Speed? Moderate. Ingenuity? MASTERFUL. Snacks stolen during the run? POSSIBLE."

The crowd howls in delight as the raccoon disappears into a tunnel like a furry shadow.

Europe's hedgehog charges forward with heroic enthusiasm—
and immediately bumps into the first hurdle.

THUP

The entire stadium goes "awwwwwww."

But the hedgehog backs up, tries again, clambers over with determination, and rolls down the next ramp in a tight little ball, gaining shocking speed before landing in foam blocks.

It shakes itself off with the dignity of someone who meant to do that.

"TECHNIQUE? UNIQUE. SPIRIT? A PERFECT TEN!" I declare proudly.

The hedgehog gets the loudest cheers so far.

The wallaby reaches the final stretch with a towering lead. It leaps into the last tunnel—
shoots out like a happy, furry missile—
SOARS over the water pit—
and lands across the finish line in an EPIC flying leap.

The stadium detonates in cheers.

"WALLABY WINS!!!" I scream as my feathers poof out in celebratory fluff. "AUSTRALIA TAKES THE—"

But suddenly—

Everything stops.

A meerkat official sprints onto the track.
Another gasps.
A third faints dramatically onto a safety mat.
A fourth frantically rewinds instant replay footage.

My heart drops.

Uh oh.

The head meerkat climbs the podium, clearing his throat like a judge preparing to deliver terrible news.

"There... has been an incident."

The stadium freezes, holding its breath.

On the big screen, the replay shows the wallaby's spectacular final tunnel launch...
and then—

As it blasts upward, its powerful feet strike the top of the foam tunnel, collapsing the structure.

According to Rule 7B:

"Tunnel structures must be passed THROUGH, not ALTERED or BROKEN."

No one blames the wallaby.
It's pure bounce energy.
But rules are rules.

"With regret," the official says, raising a paw, "Australia must be disqualified."

The stadium GASPS—
a full-body, worldwide shockwave.

My wings droop.
"What... a heartbreaking twist."

This changes EVERYTHING.

The raccoon strikes a victorious pose, looking both proud and slightly like it's planning a heist.
The hedgehog blushes and waves its tiny paws.
The wallaby bows, devastated but honorable.

North America suddenly ROCKETS back into contention. Drama level: maximum.

Official Results

Gold — North America (Raccoon)
Silver — Europe (Hedgehog)
Disqualified — Australia (Wallaby)

Updated Standings After Event 15

Continent	☆ Gold	🏅 Silver	🏅 Bronze	Total
Australia	2	0	2	8
Africa	3	4	2	19
Asia	2	3	0	12
Europe	2	2	3	13
N. America	2	5	3	19
S. America	3	0	2	11
Antarctica	1	1	2	7

"I HAVE NEVER SEEN ANYTHING LIKE THIS!" I shout, pacing wildly along my perch. "The wallaby SOARS! The raccoon TRIUMPHS! The rulebook EXPLODES! And now—NOW—we head into the final event with more drama than my nest when the in-laws are over for the holidays!"

North America and Africa are TIED with only one event to go! The entire Olympics has turned into a pressure cooker with a faulty lid.

Behind me, meerkats prepare the final arena: a sprawling forest maze filled with twisting corridors, false trails, elevation changes, cryptic markers, and at least one owl decoy wearing sunglasses.

I swallow hard.

"And tomorrow," I whisper, "everything comes down to the Navigation Race. One last test. One last chance. One last moment to claim Olympic glory."

I tighten my feathers.

"Hold on, folks. The finale is going to be LEGENDARY."

It's amazing how close predators and prey can get when the only thing chasing them is glory.

17 — THE NAVIGATION RACE

Some races end in glory.

Some end in heartbreak.

Some end with a hedgehog accidentally rolling into a hot dog cart.

But the Navigation Race—the grand finale of the Animal Olympics—
is in a category of its own.

It is the kind of race whispered about in locker rooms, carved onto ancient cave walls, and feared by athletes who once got lost in a hallway with only one door. It is legendary. It is unforgiving. It is... honestly stressing me out, and I'm not even running it.

"Welcome back, everyone," I say, my voice wobbling more than I'd like. "Coach Talon here, reporting LIVE from the grand finale of these extraordinary Games—and let me tell you, my feathers have never been more emotionally unstable."

The stadium is absolutely packed. Not a single seat is empty. Every continent watches in breathless silence as we announce the standings:

NORTH AMERICA— 19 points

AFRICA — 19 points

Everything comes down to this.

On the starting line stand our three finalists.

COACH TALON'S SCOUTING REPORT		
WILD DOG AFRICA	**ALBATROSS** ANTARCTICA	**WOLF** NORTH AMERICA
NAVIGATION: TEAMWORK AND WIDE-RANGE TRACKING **SPECIAL MOVE:** PACK PATHFINDER **FUN FACT:** EACH WILD DOG HAS A UNIQUE MIX OF SPOTS — LIKE THEY ALL SHOWED UP TO THE RACE WEARING CUSTOM JERSEYS.	**NAVIGATION:** RELIES ON WIND PATTERNS AND EARTH'S MAGNETIC FIELD **SPECIAL MOVE:** OCEAN SURVEY **FUN FACT:** CAN FLY FOR HOURS WITHOUT LANDING — THE KIND OF ATHLETE WHO SIGNS UP FOR A MARATHON AND KEEPS GOING AFTER	**NAVIGATION:** USES SCENT, MEMORY, AND TEAMWORK **SPECIAL MOVE:** HOWL GUIDE **FUN FACT:** WOLVES CAN MAP OUT TERRITORIES MILES WIDE — IMPRESSIVE FOR ANIMALS THAT DON'T CARRY NOTEBOOKS

"This is it," I murmur into my mic. "One race to decide the champion. I may need a paper bag."

The tortoise referee raises the flag.

The entire stadium holds its breath.

FWIP.

The Navigation Race begins.

Africa's wild dog rockets forward with astonishing speed, disappearing into the first set of trees before I can finish saying "And they're off!" It is all instinct and intensity—legs pumping, ears forward, utterly fearless.

"AFRICA TAKES AN EARLY LEAD!" I shout over the crowd's roar. "That wild dog runs like it has unfinished business with the concept of victory!"

The wolf follows at a steady, confident pace— its steps purposeful, its gaze moving continuously from the terrain to the sky to the faint markers hidden among the branches. There is no panic in its movements. Only focus.

Meanwhile, the albatross takes a graceful leap into the air... and glides directly over a section of the course that is absolutely not part of the race. The crowd gasps. The albatross realizes the mistake midair and circles back, flapping indignantly.

The competitors reach a fork in the trail:

Left...wide, smooth, and clearly meant for speed.

Right: narrow, shaded, barely noticeable, almost hidden by foliage.

The wild dog does not hesitate. It flies down the left path without losing momentum.

The wolf slows, examines the ground, lifts its head to test the breeze, and studies the faint angle of light sneaking through the canopy. Then, with steady confidence, it turns right.

The audience erupts with excitement.

I nearly swallow my microphone.

"The wolf is trusting instinct!" I cry. "This is navigation at its finest—no signs, no shortcuts, just raw natural awareness!"

The albatross waddles indecisively, then takes off again... in the wrong direction. Two meerkats sprint after it with directional paddles.

The wild dog tears through the straightforward portions of the course with almost reckless speed, weaving around boulders and slicing between trees like it owns the forest.

The wolf glides through the trickier sections— slipping under fallen logs, easing across uneven ground, and reading each twist of the path like it is decoding a story only it can see.

And the albatross... well... every few minutes, it reappears in a random patch of sky, as if navigating entirely based on whims.

The crowd laughs every time.

I laugh too, partly from joy and partly from panic.

Then comes the first major obstacle.

A powerful river cuts across the course. The water churns and surges, and only a handful of stones rise above the surface. No path is obvious.

The wild dog arrives first and leaps immediately onto a stone. It scrambles, struggles, regains balance, and lunges for the next. By the time it reaches the opposite bank, the audience is shrieking with admiration.

Moments later, the wolf appears.

But instead of leaping blindly, it stands still. It watches the current. It studies how leaves drift downstream. Then it steps forward with graceful precision, each paw finding the exact stone that keeps it moving with the flow rather than against it.

In three elegant moves, the wolf crosses as quickly as the wild dog—maybe faster.

"UNBELIEVABLE!" I scream. "That wasn't luck— that was instinct sharpened into ART!"

Off in the distance, the albatross attempts to fly over the river and is blown down the shoreline like a feather in a windstorm. Several meerkats deploy rescue ropes.

The last challenge is a sprawling maze of towering hedges, sharp turns, false trails, elevation shifts, and strategically placed decoy markers. It is the crown jewel of meerkat engineering and the bane of every athlete's existence.

The wild dog charges in first.

The wolf follows seconds later.

At one point, they appear neck and neck at parallel paths—visible above the hedges for only a heartbeat before disappearing again.

The stadium is shaking.

My wings are shaking.

I may actually be standing on a defibrillator.

Inside the maze, the wild dog pushes into a narrow lead, taking corner after corner with ferocious certainty.

For a moment, I worry the wolf has fallen behind too far.

Then the final fork appears.

Two routes remain:

To the left...wide, clean, and inviting.

To the right...rugged, angled, full of shadows

The wild dog darts left with total confidence.

The wolf hesitates—just for a breath—
then looks upward.

Above the maze sits a small flag atop a lookout post. It flutters at a faint angle... inconsistent with the other flags.

Only the wolf notices.

It turns right.

The stadium gasps as if a single heartbeat unites them all.

This is the moment where legends are made.

Both paths curve into the final clearing.

The wild dog bursts out first—
running flat-out, pouring everything it has into the sprint toward the finish line.

But then—

From the opposite tunnel—

The wolf emerges.

And it appears ten strides closer to the finish.

The stadium erupts in a sound louder than the Loudest Call competition.

Africa's wild dog drives forward with unstoppable determination. North America's wolf digs deep, muscles surging, claws tearing at the earth with absolute resolve.

"THIS IS IT!" I scream, wings beating wildly. "INCHES, INSTINCT, AND PURE HEART!"

The finish line rushes toward them.
The world holds its breath.

And in one magnificent, lung-bursting surge—

THE WOLF CROSSES FIRST.

By a whisker.

The stadium detonates with joy.

I fall backward off my podium.

History is made.

The wolf lifts its head and releases a proud, ringing howl. The wild dog bows respectfully, acknowledging a rival worthy of the moment. The albatross lands in a shrub and is immediately applauded by everyone for enthusiasm.

I wipe tears off my microphone.

"Ladies and gentlemen... we have witnessed the making of a legend."

Official Results

Gold – North America (Wolf)
Silver – Africa (African Wild Dog)
Bronze – Antarctica (Albatross)

Updated Standings After Event 16

Continent	☆ Gold	🥈 Silver	🥉 Bronze	Total
Australia	2	0	2	8
Africa	3	5	2	21
Asia	2	3	0	12
Europe	2	2	3	13
N. America	3	5	3	22
S. America	3	0	2	11
Antarctica	1	1	3	8

"If your heart is still beating, congratulations," I say as meerkats begin rolling out giant flags, confetti cannons, and a podium polished enough to see your reflection. "Because mine is currently doing backflips."

I fan myself with a tiny flag.

"Do NOT wander off! Up next are the Closing Ceremonies, where we crown champions, shower medals, and probably cry a lot—mostly me."

18 — THE CLOSING CEREMONIES

There are moments in life when a stadium becomes something more than a stadium. When the lights glow just a little brighter, when the cheers rumble a little deeper, and when every creature—big or small, fast or slow, loud or quiet—comes together not just to celebrate victory...

Not to celebrate themselves...but to celebrate each other.

Tonight is one of those moments.

"Ladies, gentlemen, critters of all continents," I announce with a dramatic sweep of my wing, "welcome to the CLOSING CEREMONIES of the Animal Olympics!"

Music swells.
Lights shimmer.
A suspicious amount of confetti drifts down even though I'm *positive* the meerkats weren't supposed to release any yet.

The crowd rises as seven silhouettes appear at the tunnel entrance.

It's time. Each continent sends its own champion forward.

North America

The champion steps forward first, head high, posture steady, eyes glowing with quiet pride. The gold medal around its neck gleams under the lights as the stadium roars.

I feel my voice crack.

"Our champion... the wolf of North America! A creature of instinct, intelligence, and heart!"

The wolf gives a dignified nod...
then is immediately nuzzled by three excited raccoons who rushed the track. Security gently escorts them away.

South America

Next rolls in the giant otter—quite literally rolling—spinning joyfully across the grass before popping upright and waving both paws like it's greeting distant sea fans.

"Our otter of boundless spirit!" I shout. "You made every event brighter!"

The otter blows kisses.

Some land on the wolf.

The wolf pretends not to notice.

Africa

The cheetah enters with elegant, fluid steps, each one a reminder of breathtaking speed and fierce determination. The audience rises as one.

The cheetah's eyes shimmer—not sad, not defeated, but proud.

"Africa's cheetah," I say softly. "A runner of astonishing heart. A rival worthy of the podium. A legend."

The cheetah bows deeply.

Behind it, a kangaroo accidentally hops into a tuba.

Australia

The crowd laughs as the kangaroo makes its entrance with a celebratory series of enormous bounces. It waves in excitement, hops a bit too high, bumps a light rig, and lands looking embarrassed.

"Our kangaroo brought power, joy, and the most memorable disqualification in Olympic history!" I declare.

The kangaroo shrugs and grins.

Europe

The reindeer enters with calm, measured steps, antlers decorated with delicate Olympic ribbons that sway like tiny flags.

"Europe's reindeer showed endurance, grace, and holiday spirit," I say with admiration.

The reindeer beams—then has one ribbon stolen by a mischievous otter. The otter is gently escorted back to its place.

Asia

The elephant steps forward proudly and trumpets with enough enthusiasm to rattle every confetti cannon in the stadium.

"Asia's elephant offered wisdom, strength, and... a trumpet tone that could wake the ancestors!"

A confetti cannon misfires behind us. I pretend this is absolutely normal.

Antarctica

The penguin slides in on its belly, takes an elegant glide toward the podium… and goes directly under it.

A moment later, its head pops back out.

"Antarctica's penguin!" I shout. "Proof that joy comes in all sizes—and sometimes upside-down!"

The crowd laughs and claps warmly as the penguin waddles into place.

As the seven representatives gather, the lights dim except for one spotlight that shines on them in a perfect circle.

I step forward, my feathers trembling—not from nerves this time, but from awe.

"Tonight," I begin, "we celebrate champions. But more importantly… we celebrate the incredible diversity of the animal world."

I gesture to each one:

"The wolf, with instinct sharper than moonlight."

"The giant otter, whose joy lifted us all."

"The cheetah, as swift as a heartbeat."

"The kangaroo, a living spring of power and determination."

"The reindeer, steady and strong through every challenge."

"The elephant, wise enough to lead, kind enough to inspire."

"And the penguin, proving that heart isn't measured by size."

I pause, letting the moment breathe.

"Every animal is special. Every continent brings something beautiful to the world. And every one of us—no matter our speed, strength, or style—has something extraordinary inside."

The crowd falls silent.

Then the silence becomes a wave of cheering so loud I nearly fall backward.

And then—because this is the Animal Olympics—
everything immediately descends into joyful chaos.

The elephant trumpets again, launching three confetti cannons at once. The kangaroo's celebratory bounce knocks over a spotlight. The penguin slips on the confetti and is caught by the otter, who spins dramatically with it. The wolf and cheetah share a respectful bow—two champions of instinct and speed. The reindeer tries to help organize the chaos. It absolutely does not help.

And me?

I laugh. A full, heart-deep laugh that rattles my feathers.

"Ladies and gentlemen," I shout over the happy uproar, "thank you for joining us! Remember—wherever you're from, whatever you're good at, whatever makes you YOU... the world needs it."

I raise my wing one last time.

"This is Coach Talon... signing off!"

THANK YOU!

Thank you for reading Champions of the Wild! I hope you enjoyed it. If this book made you smile, I'd love it if you left a quick positive review online. It helps other readers discover the joy of the Animal Olympics

Follow WildBookz on Facebook

If you enjoyed this book, you may also enjoy my most recent book: "67 Facts About 6-7". This book provides 67 facts that are a blast for anyone obsessed with the 67 meme.

Made in the USA
Middletown, DE
18 January 2026